SETTING THE PRISONER FREE

Setting the Prisoner Free

CHRIS AND JEAN BRISTOW

Eagle Living Ministries
HALESOWEN

Published by Eagle Living Ministries
20 Mayfield Road, Hurst Green, Halesowen
West Midlands, B62 9QW
First published 1996

ISBN 0 9527881 01

Designed and produced by Bookprint Creative Services
P.O. Box 827, BN21 3YJ, England.
Printed in Great Britain.

Contents

Preface

This book was written as a handbook, to help explain what is meant by inner healing for the average Christian to understand. It is not a highly theological book nor is it meant to be! The aim was that as you understand more about what the Lord is doing in your life you can begin to recognise weaknesses and start to deal with them yourself, rather than seek out a counsellor. Obviously there is sometimes a need for us to receive prayer ministry or counselling but there is a great deal we can do to help ourselves, and so prevent more attacks from the enemy.

Since starting on this book the Holy Spirit has moved in a very dramatic way both in England and other countries. The wonderful thing about this move of the Spirit is that it is a move of God for the individual and God is speaking to people and opening up their lives to inner healing and to a heart relationship with him. Is this book necessary then? We think 'yes'! We need to understand what is happening both to ourselves and to others, for we could be in danger of criticizing or misunderstanding what God is doing. Also we need to be aware that Satan is at work too and will counterfeit all that the Holy Spirit does. It is therefore very important that we seek to be more like Jesus and look to him first and foremost in our lives. We pray this will happen to you as you read; that you will have a greater desire to seek the Lord first in your life and give him areas in which you know there is still need for improvement. We never stop needing him; indeed the last chapter of this book reveals the ways God has dealt with us over the last few months as we have sought to be holy as he is holy.

May the Lord touch your spirit as you read and may your heart be open to receive from the Lord himself so that he can speak to you through the testimonies and the teaching. Many of the testimonies are our own. Those which concern others are given with their full permission.

I

Spiritual Warfare

The army that we represent is a sick army; it's an army that has fallen by the wayside, an army that's not even dressed properly for the battle. This is the picture that the Lord showed me. It's also an exhausted army, and the reason it is exhausted is because those who are ready for battle are worn out hanging on to those who are not ready. That is why we cannot reach the unconverted in the world—we are so busy trying to take care of one another. So we have a picture of an exhausted, half-dressed army; one that is weak and wounded, not by the enemy so much as by what we have done to one another: the way we have talked about each other, the way we have wounded and hurt each other, because we have rendered each other powerless by the words we have spoken.

The Lord showed me what a sad picture we have given to the world of the army of God. It's not the sort of army we would expect God to use.

This is, however, the army God wants to use to conquer the world.

How then can we improve this situation? This book has been written to help you deal with yourself, so that knowing what to do, you can have a life that is ongoing and victorious. You can learn to fight the true enemy rather than one another, and hence hurting one another, for this is the army that God said would take over the world. You know, God can do it without us! He does not really need us, yet he has chosen to use us and revival is

only going to come when we as a people learn how to deal
with ourselves and how to cope with one another and how
to love one another. The Holy Spirit more than ever before
is revealing the true self in this day and age, and we need
to understand what is happening.

The Scriptures in Ephesians 6 are words that many of us
will know, but let us refresh ourselves and be reminded of
what The Lord is saying through the apostle Paul: 'Finally,
be strong in the Lord and in his mighty power' (v. 10). Not
in our own strength, but in the Holy Spirit's power. We
cannot reach out without the power of the Holy Spirit in
our lives.

Look at verse 11: 'Put on the full armour of God so that
you can take your stand against the devil's schemes.'

I found this verse quite interesting when I was praying
about it. There are a lot of Christians who think that when
they accept Jesus into their lives as Saviour, from then on
they have the armour of God. This is true, but let me
explain how they have it. If you enrol into the State
Army, you go for an interview and, if you are accepted,
you sign on the dotted line. You are then handed a pile of
clothes, your uniform, made to measure and ready for use,
for you to put on. The next command you are given is to
put the uniform on.

That is what happens at salvation. Jesus says in
effect, 'Here is your armour beautifully laid out for
you, but you have to put it on.' God gives it to you
freely. It's all part of the salvation package, but you
have to put it on.

There are three obvious situations where the Scriptures
clearly tells us to put on the armour. When we first accept
Jesus into our lives we need to put on the full armour so
that we can stand against the enemy: 'For our struggle is
not against flesh and blood, but against . . . the powers of
this dark world and against the spiritual forces of evil in
the heavenly realms. Therefore put on the full armour of
God, so that when the day of evil comes, you may be able

to stand your ground, and after you have done everything, to stand' (vv. 12–13).

Secondly, we are told: 'Therefore put on the full armour of God, so that when the day of evil comes, you may be able to stand your ground.' Is this not the evil day? Are we not up against evil today more than ever before? So if we have to stand in our armour when we accept Christ, how much more must we stand in the evil day of today.

Thirdly, another situation when we must stand is when we cannot do anything else: 'After you have done everything, to stand' (v. 13). Is not that the time when we want to give up? God is asking us to stand when there is nothing else we can do—when we have come to the end of ourselves. We are told to stand and then God will come and minister to us through the Holy Spirit. Why is it then that from the picture we see of the Christian church we are not continuing to stand?

I want you to picture a landing strip. If you have an aircraft, it isn't much good to you if it cannot land. An aircraft needs a landing strip on which to land safely. Let's imagine that Satan has an aircraft full of fiery darts. Now if he has nowhere to land then he cannot operate. In fact he's rendered useless. But if he can find a place to land then he can do his worst. Where does he look to land? He looks not in the world but in the Christian. He looks for your weaknesses and where you are not doing what God has asked you to do, that becomes a landing strip for Satan.

Therefore each of you must put off falsehood and speak truthfully to his neighbour, for we are all members of one body. 'In your anger do not sin': Do not let the sun go down while you are still angry, and do not give the devil a foothold [or landing strip]. He who has been stealing must steal no longer, but must work, doing something useful with his own hands, that he may have something to share with those in need. Do not let any unwholesome talk come out of your mouths, but only what is helpful for building others up according to their needs, that it may benefit those who listen. And do not grieve the Holy Spirit of God, with whom you were sealed for the day of redemption. Get rid of all bitterness, rage and anger, brawling and slander, along with every form of malice. Be kind and compassionate to one another, forgiving each other, just as in Christ God forgave you (Eph 4:25–32).

That passage was not written to non-Christians. It was written to the children of God, or as the heading in my Bible says 'The Children of the Light'. So that is how we as Christians need to live; and one of the reasons my husband and I felt very strongly that we should write this book is because we want to see the church living according to the Scripture, and Christians able to cope with the problems of today.

We will share more fully about the landing strips in the next chapters. There are many of them. Some, we find, have a root in sin; some are emotional weaknesses, many of which are not our own fault–they have been put on us by some hurt or wound that as yet has not been recognised. Hopefully as you read and start to think about what God is saying to you, the Holy Spirit will reveal to you places in your own life where you need to be aware of the enemy being able to land. Be encouraged that the truth can set you free.

We need protection against Satan's fiery darts. Every one of us has weak spots. When I was a young Christian, church seemed to be portrayed as a group of people who were very good and never did wrong. That is not how we are. We are human beings. We have got weaknesses and if we confess and recognise our weaknesses then we can help one another. As I write this I can assure you that both my husband Chris and I would acknowledge we have weaknesses, and in the next few chapters we shall be sharing some of those with you. What we have learned is to recognise where they are, and we have also learned how to cope with them and deal with them so that they do not cause lasting harm by being a permanent landing strip for the enemy to play havoc with us.

The following are some of the things we are sharing about in this first chapter that we hope will be helpful.

1. The need for protection for our weak spots.
2. The need for discipline in our lives to do things God's way.
3. The need to examine ourselves in the light of the 'foothold' or 'landing strip' and to recognise the sin, wound or hurt.

Let us look first of all at the armour and see where we are not fully dressed, and hence where the enemy is able to land.

We start with the helmet of salvation. I am sure many people think this never comes off–after all, it is the helmet of salvation–but that is not completely true. The helmet of salvation is given to us for protection and we can only use it if we are Christians; non-Christians have no helmet of salvation. The helmet is on top of the pile that was given to you when you accepted Christ, and you can take it off and on at will. The Scripture clearly commands us to 'put on the whole armour of God'. Therefore you have a free will to put on and take off this helmet of protection.

We could tell you many stories and illustrations of when we take the helmet off, but this is just an introduction and it will be dealt with more fully later.

The helmet protects our mind and it is in our minds that Satan is trying to work, in our thought-life. We will be dealing with a lot of this in the chapter on sexual problems, because it is our thought-life that suffers when the helmet is off and Satan has been able to get in and play havoc with our minds. We have then blamed the enemy, which is not the true picture. We have been given a helmet to protect us, and if we have taken if off then we are at fault, and what we need to recognise is that we have a responsibility to God. We can choose whether or not to put the armour on and wear it. Whenever you listen to those unclean thoughts, to those words or criticism and hurt, you are in danger of taking off the helmet and need to put it back.

When you realise you have been listening to the enemy this is what you need to do. First, confess your sin and tell the Lord you are sorry. 'I've sinned and let you down.' You then renounce whatever it was you heard, whatever it was that you listened to which was unclean or hurtful and not of God, renounce it and say something like: 'I renounce that unclean thought that came into my head and I refuse to listen.' It is always best if you can name the sin specifically. You will then receive the forgiveness of the heavenly Father. Ask for the protection of Jesus and the power of the Holy Spirit to keep you, and above all forgive yourself for listening in the first place, otherwise you will land up in guilt and condemnation, and that is not what God wants.

Finally, you will need to receive healing for the wound sustained, and we will be learning in this book how to receive forgiveness and healing, and about others who have witnessed that God has set them free from landing strips that the enemy had in their lives. The pattern of repenting, renouncing, receiving forgiveness and healing will come up over and over again until it becomes part of our lives. Hopefully we will learn to recognise the voice of the enemy and renounce it before he can land, saving ourselves sometimes weeks of agony.

This then is an ongoing battle; it is not something you do once at salvation. I am having constantly to renounce thoughts, and he does not give up easily. When defeated, he will look for another area in which to attack us. We need to be constantly on our guard and to realise that we have a Saviour who at salvation gave us a helmet for our protection and we need to keep it on. We will only do this by the pattern of repenting and renouncing; that is, nipping it in the bud! For out of our thought-life all else stems. We are what we think and thinking is the next stage after hearing, for we then dwell on what we have heard. It's not a sin to be tempted, but it is a sin to dwell on it and start the seed of sin germinating. Eventually the enemy will give up and leave us alone in that area, but we have a responsibility in the battle, to allow the Lord to fight for us and use the armour he has given us. We need to wage warfare until the fiery darts stop. Satan will then say, 'Here is a Christian who means business. I'm not going to waste my time.' But beware! Don't feel proud of your victory because the victory belongs to Jesus and was won for you on the cross. And Satan will be back!

What else is there that need protection? Needless to say, our bodies! The fiery darts affect us through our bodies. Further on in this book we shall show you how the mind is attacked first and then the body. We have on the body the breastplate of righteousness. If you sin with your mind, this nearly always leads to acts carried out by the body, and the breastplate will no longer be in operation. At salvation we were given the garments of righteousness because we were cleansed by the precious blood of Jesus, but we are continually soiling our garments. So again we need to go through the pattern of confessing, repenting and receiving forgiveness.

When we come to the human spirit, the belt of truth is a great help to us when attacked. John 8:32 says: 'The truth will set you free.'

If you start to learn the truth about yourself, the words of Scripture can enable you to be set free as you use them to confront the enemy as Jesus did. As you learn to keep short accounts, you will begin to realise where Satan is attacking, and begin to deal with him quickly as you recognise the area of attack where the arrows are hurting and wounding you, instead of leaving it for days and sometimes months. (We have had people who have come to us after months and even years of attack. If only they had realised where the area of attack was, they could have dealt with it within seconds, when the thought started to be bedded into their mind.) It is a matter of learning to keep short accounts so that the armour is worn almost continually as we confess, repent and receive the healing forgiveness of Jesus.

I would like to share with you a little testimony from my own life that will help you to see how the truth really does set you free. A few years ago I was receiving some prayer ministry for my fear of flying. We prayed about it and then I was asked how long I had had this fear. It seemed to me that it had been with me a very long time and yet I had never flown, so why fear something I had not had to do? It was as we discussed it that I realised it was not just flying, but it was also connected to a fear of being shut in confined spaces; and as we were praying the Lord began to show me pictures of something that had happened to me when I was a small child.

One day I was playing quite happily in the garden shed. I often played in the shed and this particular day was a Sunday. In those days the front room of the house was kept for Sunday use only and my mother was entertaining a friend in the front of the house. I was quite happy playing with my dolls when suddenly the garden shed door closed and I was in the dark and could not open the door.

My cries for help were in vain as my mother was in the front room. I have no idea how long I cried or how long it took for panic and fear to grip me, but in my desperation to get out of my prison, I climbed through a window into a chicken shed which was adjoining the shed I was in and escaped through the chicken house door. But of course by this time I was in a bad way and it took a lot of consoling by my parents before I could explain what had happened.

The fear of being shut in remained with me almost up to the present day and it wasn't until I asked for prayer for the fear of flying that the truth dawned on me. So we prayed and asked the Lord to deal with the fear. I used the pattern of first confessing my part in allowing the arrow of fear to get into my mind and then we asked God to fill the places with his love and healing. You see fear is a fiery dart, an enemy attack, and even though I was a child and all those years had gone by, I still needed to confess my fear and renounce it because it still had a hold on my life. Then I could receive the forgiveness of the Lord because 'perfect love casts out fear'.

Of course I had to wait until I was going on a plane to work out my healing, but I did not have to wait long because we felt the Lord was leading us to get involved in prayer counselling in Northern Ireland, so my first flight was to Belfast! It was not the place I would have chosen for my first flight, but I know that when God heals it is complete, and I enjoyed every minute of the flight because the fear had been taken away and no longer had a hold on me.

I trust sharing that with you will encourage you that once you see the pattern of where the enemy is attacking, you can apply the principles of healing to your own life. We will see this too in the other areas that are shared in this book.

So the belt of truth can set you free, by knowing yourself and knowing the truth about Scripture, which you can use as a weapon in the same way as Jesus did when Satan tried to tempt him.

Any deviation from the truth harms our standing as a soldier, and today we need to be so much on our guard because there are many religious sects that have deviated from the truth. If we belong to or have any association with any sect that is not standing for the truth, we will never be set free until we have renounced our dealings with them. So ask the Holy Spirit to reveal the truth to you and especially if you have doubt in your heart about the group you belong to.

We also have weapons of defence and attack. The shield of faith needs to be held up to deflect the fiery darts. Here is a list of some of the darts that attack us. This is by no means all of them for there are thousands, but perhaps these reveal some of the most common.

Depression	Idolatry	Lying	Pride
Fear	Unclean thoughts	Covetousness	Perfection
Anger	Lust	Manipulation	
Hatred	Control		

We have a shield of faith and we need to use it to stop the darts from reaching us. That is a scriptural plea to us as Christians to be disciplined in our use of the shield of faith and to recognise that Jesus is able to keep us from falling.

When we stand together we can interlock our shields to provide more protection; and we will be explaining later about how important relationships are. Friends–you need friends. Not people who will let you down, but people you can trust who will provide safe places for you to share. I trust that in our church we are providing such places where we can have the confidence of knowing that what we are sharing is kept secret between us. We need that safe place where we can share because we cannot live the Christian life on our own. If we keep ourselves to ourselves, we will struggle and the whole army will be affected. We need one another if we are to reach out into the world.

We also need to confess our faults to one another, but we must confess in wisdom. Chris and I would be very careful who we confessed to. We certainly would not go to someone who after we had shared was on the phone saying, 'You'll never guess what the pastor has been doing!' It would not be helpful to us or to God. We look for people we know we can trust and we are blessed by having a group of Christians we can share with. I can ring them up at any time and seek prayer and help.

We need also to use the sword of the Spirit. It's no good you seeking help if you are not reading God's word. This is where discipline comes in. God's word is there not only for you to read and digest but to use as a weapon of warfare.

Think how many times Jesus used the Scriptures to send Satan packing. Jesus had fiery darts thrown at him, but he had no weaknesses, no landing strips. He knows we have weaknesses and he has given us the armour to help us, and he has told us to put it on and use it. If we do not use it then we have only ourselves to blame. It's our own fault. Some Christians walk around blaming the enemy for everything and never consider that they may be to blame.

If we allow Satan to get in, then we are responsible, and until we recognise our responsibility for our own sin we will not be set free. We will not therefore stand in the evil day and and having done all stand. As an army we often stand divided—Satan robs us and renders us powerless. We gain nothing by this, but as we seek reconciliation we begin to claim back our inheritance in Christ.

The Christian army is the only army that deliberately wounds its friends. There are many wounded and isolated Christians up and down our land who are not in relationship because they have been hurt and wounded so much that they fear another pain. We ourselves have also been in that position and would plead with you to receive the healing of Jesus. We can never stop being hurt, but we can understand how to receive healing and forgiveness that will set us free and enable us to stand once again. Don't allow another Christian to rob you of your healing in Christ, giving Satan satisfaction. Renounce the words of the enemy and refuse to be in that position any more. If you honestly have no one to turn to, then let us put you in touch with a Christian who is trustworthy.

When revival comes we shall be so concerned with our own lives and making sure we are not sinning that we will not have time to bother with our brother's faults. Rather we will receive each other with true love and repentance. We want to get to a place of acceptance of one another as Jesus accepts us, and learn to walk free, making sure our own prayer-life and our own walk with Jesus are right first.

On 10th January 1995 we were still in Toronto and my husband Chris received the following prophetic word from the Lord, which he shared at the intercessors' meeting. We believe this should now be added to the end of this chapter.

'I saw a large pearl against a dark background, then being joined by smaller beautiful pearls, tear-shaped and full of shining lustre, strung together. The impression was that behind the pearl necklace were old-fashioned methods of diving without apparatus, involving time, hardship, perils, suffering and tears; that somehow the sufferings of Christ and the painful life experiences of ourselves came together to shape our character and wonderfully transform it, and that we were strung together by the unifying cord of the Holy Spirit until we were one, and then the light of the glorious gospel of Jesus would shine with full splendour and power. I felt the Lord's heart for unity in his church and that hardship would bring us together, for divided we fall but united we stand.'

2

Shame and Humiliation

Shame first entered the world way back in Genesis, almost at the very beginning of time. When God created man and woman they were in perfect relationship with their Creator God. We read in Genesis 2:25 that they were 'both naked, and they felt no shame.' They were free from shame.

The mention of shame at the end of creation in chapter 2 is very significant to the whole world. We know of course that in chapter 3 the cunning old serpent creeps and crawls to chat up the woman Eve and pulls the wool over her eyes in many respects, but what she should have done was call for her husband to help! Since Adam was supposed to be a gardener, why did he leave a hole in his fence for this stranger to get in? It's obvious that when the woman saw the tree of good and evil it was a delight to her eyes, and being encouraged by the serpent she took of the fruit and ate. It tasted so good, and she in turn encouraged her husband to take and eat. Then the eyes of both were opened, and they knew that they were naked.

The first mention we have of nakedness before this is in connection with not being ashamed. The logic is that when they actually realised they were naked then they became ashamed because the first thing they did when they were in this state was to cover their nakedness. They grabbed big fig leaves and sewed them together to cover themselves. The meaning of the word 'shame' is 'to cover', and when you have a feeling of being ashamed, the thing you want to

19

do is to hide it in some way because you have been
exposed to an experiece that you do not like very much.

Adam and Eve felt guilty, because in the cool of the
evening God came, as he always did, and they hid themselves from him, full of guilt. God called, 'Where are
you?' Of course God knew where they were, but he
wanted them to respond. They said they were afraid, but
where had fear come in? Fear is associated with shame
and with sin. They confessed their sin and were thrown out
of the garden feeling guilty and ashamed, and that guilt
and shame has been inbred into mankind ever since. It has
never gone away; nor has condemnation, nor has guilt and
nor has sin. The serpent has not gone away and neither has
human nature.

The significant thing about us all today is that we have
covered our bodies with clothes, which is the very thing
Adam and Eve did to cover their guilt. We would feel
ashamed if our bodies were exposed to one another.
Shame therefore is very significat in healing. The good
news is that God can deal with shame, and the even better
news is that he can turn it round to produce humility and
blessing. If you have had an experience of shame or a
history of being ashamed, be encouraged that everything
can work together for good to those who are called, as
Romans 8:28 states. We need to allow God to heal those
areas that cause us to be hurt or cause obstacles in our
relationships, and to bring those areas to the foot of the
cross. When Jesus said, 'It is finished!' it meant he could
bring an end to your shame and humiliation. In the same
way that sin is finished at the cross, so also are shame and
humiliation . . . praise God!

There are two types of shame. The first kind is that
which produces humility, and we all need to be humble
before God. We have no righteousness of our own by
which we can earn his grace or favour. The type of shame
we are talking about here is that which is malevolent; it is
destructive; it causes humiliation; it causes us to lose our

self-worth; it cripples our walk with God and handicaps our ability to function and operate properly. It causes a variety of feelings, including confusion and lack of self-esteem. I know this to be true as I have been on the receiving end and will share about this later on.

Let us define shame. What does the dictionary say? 'Shame is that intense experience of self-rejection that happens or comes with unexpected exposure to one's diminished self.' To this I add my own explanation. This self-rejection carries with it the feeling of loathing, despair, hatred and lack of self-acceptance. One dictionary defines it as 'a painful sensation excited by the exposure of that which nature or modesty prompts us to conceal, or by a consciousness of guilt or having done something that injures our reputation and person or self-worth or value, often causing confusion'.

When we are ashamed we do not like who we are and we wish we were a thousand miles away where no one knows us. The good news is that shame was dealt with at the cross. Jesus is able to heal.

The following is a true case history of a healing that took place. Please be assured that this and all case studies are given with the permission of the person involved and all names are changed to protect identity.

We will call the little girl Jenny. She was about five years old and attending infant school, but she had a real problem that affected her whole life and filled her with fear. She could never ask to go to the toilet and always went home wet. As far as she could remember she had had this problem, right from potty training. The difficulty that loomed ahead in her mind was facing her mum when she went home. She loved her mum, but dreaded her finding out about her wet clothes. It would mean a smack or, worse than that, the humiliation of having her face rubbed in the wet underwear. In her little mind she devised ways of hiding her clothes or creeping in and trying to wash them herself, but, she was always found out.

After several months at school the problem seemed to clear up, but the shame and the humiliation that had come into her life would not go away. She grew up always trying to please others, being obedient in order to try and gain acceptance and therefore escape chastisement. In her school work, and later her work in the world, she found herself wanting to please and having real problems when things went against her. The same feelings of shame and humiliation rose to the surface and she would want to run and hide herself away. Even as a Christian she had great difficulty with acceptance, and needed always to be doing something for Jesus.

One day during a talk on healing she recognised her problem and in a counselling session the root was found: the early years of severe punishment had damaged her emotions. The root was exposed and forgiveness of Mum and of self were dealt with. Also the recognition of a sin of deceit was confessed. The shame and humiliation were then brought to the cross and the love of Jesus was prayed into the wounds and the hurt of the little girl. When this was all done it brought about a wonderful healing and release of the true person who could now freely know she was accepted by her Saviour, and was now free to serve him and not always be at the beck and call of others.

Let us look at some verses that show us how Jesus dealt with our shame. In Hebrews 12:2 it says that Jesus 'endured the cross, despising the shame' (RSV). The cross deals with sin, but here Jesus endures the cross while despising the shame, and is seated at the right hand of God. We know that the first occasion that he sits at the right hand of God is when he made purification for our sins. It says in Hebrews 1:3 that he 'upholds the universe by his word of power' (RSV). Interesting that in the two mentions of the right hand of God, which is the seat of power, one is purification for sins and the other is turning his back on shame.

Then in Isaiah 53:3–6 it says that Jesus bore our shame and suffering. If you look at the passage it is obvious that what the prophet is describing is not just shameful behaviour but one who is suffering shame: 'And we esteemed him not ... yet we esteemed him stricken smitten by God, and afflicted. ... But he was wounded for our transgressions ... and with his stripes we are healed' (RSV). That was a shameful experience, and if you look in the New Testament you find that in every gospel narrative of the crucifixion the crowds mocked, the soldiers jeered and spat in his face, whipped and bruised his back and nailed him to the cross. All this adds up to a cruel, shameful and humiliating experience. Then to make things even worse, the soldiers gambled his clothes while the religious leaders shouted at him, 'He can save others, so why doesn't he save himself?' and, 'Why, don't you prophesy who it is who is smiting you on the cheek?' He endured shame. I think if that had been me I would not have coped. To be the object of everyone's hatred and mockery is something that would reduce my self-worth and acceptance and evaluation of myself right down to ground level. Psalm 22:6 says: 'I am a worm and not a man.' It means that the psalmist felt like a worm. I would encourage you to read Psalm 22 and also Colossians 2:14–15: 'Having cancelled the written code ... he took it away, nailing it to the cross. And having disarmed the powers and authorities, he made a public spectacle of them, triumphing over them by the cross.' If Jesus can defeat the powers and authorities, he can defeat the shame that you have experienced. That is good news.

A verse of an old hymn we used to sing states this:

> Bearing shame and scoffing rude
> In my place condemned He stood
> Sealed my pardon with his blood
> Hallelujah, what a Saviour.

There is a tremendous exchange that is made at the cross. I give him my sin; he gives me his life. I give him my life and my death; he gives me his resurrection life. I give him my problems; he gives me his peace. I give him my shame; he gives me his sense of well-being. I give him my grief; he gives me his joy. I give him my hurt and rejection; he gives me his love and aceptance. It's the most marvellous transactions the world has ever known. This deal is guaranteed and you cannot lose. We should advertise this for all to hear. The heart of it is that if you love someone so much, you will give then everything, and God loved us so much he gave us his Son that we might be free in every way.

The first time I realised what had happened to me regarding shame in my life it was like hearing a telephone bell going off in my mind. I knew God was touching me in a way I had not experienced before. I was in a very important meeting at the time, so I put the handcuffs on my feelings until I could get home and be in a quiet place, and I then unlocked the handcuffs and what came out was tears and tears and still more tears for several hours. You see, I know what it is like to be on the receiving end of feeling shame.

Let's have a look at what happens to us in shame. Shame brings exposure to ourselves. That's what shame brings. We feel exposed, with nowhere to run. It can be seen what we think we are really like because it takes hold of us so completely. Self-consciousness then takes over as we realise what we should be like, how repulsive we must look, what an idiot we must be. Everyone must know. What must they think of us? We're a failure and will not be wanted.

It can also lead to terror, or fear and anxiety. These are not feelings we have received in Jesus: 'God did not give us a spirit of timidity, but a spirit of power, of love and of self-discipline' (2 Tim 1:7)

In a shame attack we are full of self-consciousness and fear, and sometimes we are paralysed with fear and do not know what to say or do. Do you know what one of the dreadful shame attacks on me was? It was when my first son was a year old and critically ill and I did not know what to do or what to say. I prayed, but I was helpless and I had this terrible fear in my gut and my mind froze. By the time we got him to the hospital he had died.

That is a terrible thing to live with when you look back and you realise perhaps you could have done more, but shame had taken over so that the thing you could have done you didn't do and the thing you should have said you couldn't say. It strips you naked and your reaction is to run and hide and cover. Is that not what Adam and Eve did? I will hide away so that it will not happen again and then anger sets in at myself. Why did I act that way? Why did I not do more? Simon, our son, had been visited by the doctor, who told us to leave him a day to get better, but deep down we wanted to ignore her advice and go to the hospital, but fear stood in our way. Why didn't I ignore what the doctor was saying and go to the hospital myself instead of waiting? There were other reasons for my reaction, but the whole incident left me ashamed.

In another completely different situation I felt the rage of shame. I had another girlfriend before my wife–a few in fact! This particular girlfriend came to me one day and told me it was all off and she was going out with a married man who was getting a divorce. I was so angry and humiliated by the situation. I felt thrown out like some old sock with a hole in it; discarded; no use. I hid myself away, but at the end of it I was so angry. I nearly smashed the door down with my fists as I came to terms with my feelings for this other man.

Don't tell me you do not have times like this in your life. You may not express it clearly and be willing to expose yourself as to how you feel, but deep down inside you know that what I am saying is speaking to you. You have felt angry. The Scripture says: 'Be angry and do not sin,' and I had to repent of my anger and take it to the cross. When I did that, God gave me someone far better who has given me twenty-nine years of faithfulness, not someone who would throw me away like an old slipper or sock. She loves me and accepts me.

Sometimes this shame reaction will last just a few minutes, but sometimes it lasts days or even years. Every shame has to begin somewhere. It might have begun at home when you were with your brothers and sisters, or at school when you were shamed or humiliated and you were dragged out in front of the class because you were accused unfairly of cheating and copying someone's work. That is enough to shame a child for life and many have had experiences like that. Or it may be with your grandparents–a look or a word or an action that affected you from then on. It doesn't matter where it began. It becomes a spider's web of shame, woven together so that if you touch the web in one part with your finger the whole web shakes.

This is what happens when shame is not healed. No matter where you are touched in the present, the whole of your past experieces will come to the surface; the whole fabric of your structure will be shaken and may render you incapable of acting–as in the case of our son's sickness–or make you very angry–as in the case of my old girlfriend. So similar events or similar circumstances can re-awaken the shame pattern of the past with frightful speed. That is why we cannot cope with it unless we break the pattern. The truth is, we can be shame-based people.

I want to share a story here that I have permission to share, as told by a young Christian. This is the type of story you may well share round the dinner table and have a good laugh about, but it also has other more serious implications.

'As a small child I was brought up in Malta and the blocks of flats that we lived in had steps leading up to them from the pavement. There was a huge wall in front of the flats so we had a wall, steps leading up to the front door and then wall again. The wall was about 6 feet high and provided a lovely backdrop for the Maltese ladies to sit on the steps and place baskets of food. For us children the wall was a wonderful place to play follow my leader and all the children would follow the one at the front and do exactly what he or she did.

'I was only three years old at that time and as I was the smallest and the youngest I was always at the end of the line. This particular day we were all walking along the top of the wall, singing away, not a care in the world, when we decided to jump off the wall onto the pavement. Then it came to my turn.

'It just so happened that a Maltese lady was sitting on the steps selling baskets of eggs. So along I came. I got to the end and being the smallest the others offered to help me down. But as I was the youngest I insisted on jumping on my own and landed up in the middle of a large basket of eggs.

'You can imagine the excitement that followed. The Maltese lady was flying her arms around in anger, the children were screaming with delight and I was hauled off to my mum by the other children, who proceeded to explain what I had done. The lady waving her arms in the air followed close behind and my mum had to pay for the damage, and I was not allowed to forget it. The song that rang through our house was eggs for breakfast, eggs for tea, eggs for supper and still more eggs.

'That was the first time I encountered shame, and so many incidents have happened since when I have run away rather that have to confront or be exposed. Even in meetings when we have been asked to go round a circle and introduce ourselves my hands would start to shake, my heart would beat fast and I would feel an absolute failure and lost for words. Afterwards I would feel so angry with myself and feel a complete failure. My immediate reaction would be that I was never going to do that again.'

It is lovely to see the change that healing from shame has made for this young Christian, who is now so supportive in

the church and competent in many ways, simply by
recognising the shame pattern in her life and receiving
forgiveness and acceptance from Jesus. So even what
seems like a minor incident can affect a child for the
rest of their life if not dealt with.

There are three main types of response to remove
shame. First, you can become a people-pleaser, always
doing what others say in order to become accepted. Here
you reduce your shame by recognition and hence being
loved. This is only achieved by works, so you work harder
to please. If you do things to please, then you will not be
humiliated or exposed. This is a very familiar pattern in
many people and it is a treadmill of works to please. You
move towards people to please them because if you please
them you will not be put to shame. If you stay in their
good books they will not say or do anything that will add
to your shame.

Secondly, you can move away from people. You can
become isolated, putting a wall around yourself so that
you can't be shamed any more; making a decision that you
will go through life alone; you do not need the help of
others. If you have no relationships then no one will be
able to say anything that will shame you again. This is not
what God intended for us.

Thirdly, you move against people; you become work- or
performance-orientated, always proving yourself so you
can feel good about yourself, and since no one can find
fault with your work, no one can find fault with you either.

All of us have a tendency to one of these categories or a
combination of two of them.

Baptism in the Holy Spirit or a use of the gifts does
not heal shame. You will meet people who have a
spiritual gift but definitely fall into one of these categories. Moving in the Holy Spirit's power is no guaran-
tee that you will be healed of your shame. The only way
to be freed from your shame is to give it to God and let
him deal with it.

In Matthew 18:3 it speaks of receiving the kingdom of God as a child, in simplicity and trust. The main point I want to emphasise is that there is a child still within you. Understand that your childhood experiences moulded you to become the adult you are now. You have been shaped by the past.

If we look in Luke's Gospel, chapter 5, we find that Jesus gets into a boat. It's Simon's boat and Jesus wants to be pushed out a little from the land to get away so that he can teach the people from the water (voices carry over water). When Jesus had finished speaking he said to Simon 'Push out into the deep and let your net down for a chatch.' Simon then answered Jesus (I wonder how he said this!): 'Master, we have toiled all night and have caught nothing, but at your word we will let down the nets.' Simon was not happy. He acted like a people-pleaser—'At your word I will let down the nets.' He actually felt like a failure. He had fished all night and had caught nothing. He was going to lose out with no fish to sell. It was a shameful thing for a fisherman not to catch any fish. Peter did not really want to go fishing because he had failed, but nevertheless he let down the nets to please Jesus. Jesus had a word of knowledge and he asked Peter to act upon it. When Peter saw the result he had a shame attack: 'Depart from me. I am a sinful man.' He wanted to run and hide. He did not want to be exposed.

If Jesus could see into the water, what could he see in the heart and mind of Peter? What can he see in us?

Peter could not cope with this and became fearful, hence his reaction to want to hide. Jesus loved Peter and knew he had not caught anything, so he gave Peter the biggest catch of his whole life, but Peter could not cope with it and accept it.

A person who is ashamed cannot receive unearned love. If you are a people-pleaser you have to do something to earn love. Unconditional love cannot be received, so when you come across a person who works and works yet cannot

receive love with no strings attached, then behind it all
you will find a shameful experience at the root. Peter
thought he was too evil and could not cope with the
love he was shown by Jesus. How did Jesus know the
fish were in the deep when all fishermen know these fish
only live in the shallows? How much does he know about
me?

How then can we be released and healed from shame?
We need to think differently about it. Jesus despised
shame. He looked down on it. He did not let it overwhelm
him. Here is a pattern we can adopt for ourselves.

First, we confess our shame to God. We cannot cope
with it; we need to hand it over. Then, secondly, we need
to forgive those who have shamed us. This may be
difficult. I did not find it easy to forgive my girlfriend.
The only thing unforgiveness will do is make us sick.
Thirdly, let us repent of our negative response. We may
have been an innocent victim, but we need to repent of our
reaction, whether it be to run, or to hide away in fear. We
then clear the ground for the enemy not to exploit the
situation.

We then need to renounce this shame; rebuke it. We do
not want it; it's a bother. Find a text that will build up your
faith–a text that has something about you in it, as being
beautiful, accepted, loved, wanted, a child of God. You
need to find scripture that tells you you are a worthwhile
person and that Jesus died and removed your shame, and
to agree with what you read. You are not a worm; you do
not wriggle (only under pressure)! Do not as a Christian
belittle yourself, for you were made in the image of God
and you are not worthless. Jesus died for you because he
loved you and thought you were worth dying for. He died
to make you a king or a priest or a son or daughter of the
living God.

You need to rewrite the script that you have written
about yourself of who and what you are in God. Then be
willing to let God love you. Some are not willing to let

God love them. Let me say that again: let God love you. Receive his love.

Some will be like Lazarus and need to remove the old grave clothes. They have the resurrection life but are bound by the patterns of the past and therefore may need the help of someone they know and trust to help them break free. In the case of Lazarus it was bandages, but in their case it will be bondages that will bind them and they will need prayer to release them. This does mean they run the risk of exposure. However, sometimes we cannot free ourselves but need help and healing from another.

What we can do for ourselves is to renew our minds, read the Scriptures and allow the truth to sink into our minds. We should encourage one another in relationships where we will not be let down, and let God love us and renew us in his love. We must believe the Lord will answer our prayers.

So, in a nutshell, we have three A's: Ask the Spirit to come; Allow him to deal with your shame; Accept his healing and God will come and will do a work in you of healing and freedom from shame and humiliation.

I could share many testimonies of people who have been set free including our own testimony. God is able to heal all situations, and no circumstances, however shameful to us, are a problem to him.

3

Emotional and Sexual Problems

In Galatians 5:19–26 we read this:

> The acts of the sinful nature are obvious: sexual immorality,
> impurity and debauchery; idolatry and witchcraft; hatred,
> discord, jealousy, fits of rage, selfish ambition, dissensions,
> factions and envy; drunkenness, orgies, and the like. I warn
> you, as I did before, that those who live like this will not
> inherit the kingdom of God. But the fruit of the Spirit is love,
> joy, peace, patience, kindness, goodness, faithfulness, gentle-
> ness and self-control. Against such things there is no law.
> Those who belong to Christ Jesus have crucified the sinful
> nature with its passions and desires. Since we live by the
> Spirit, let us keep in step with the Spirit. Let us not become
> conceited, provoking and envying each other.

This is just an introduction on emotional healing as we
will write more in future chapters. As we mentioned in
Chapter 1, we do have landing strips in our lives that the
enemy uses, and one of these landing strips is our emotions, especially when damaged. We can continually be
attacked and often not know why. We are made up of
body, mind and spirit, and in that make-up our emotions
play an important role.

How often we hear in counselling words like: 'It is not
fair. My life has been destroyed. I have been robbed of
my childhood.' People have come for help who have
been abused and crippled emotionally for years. One
question that always has to be answered is: Why does
God allow it to happen in the first palce? Although this

chapter is not meant to be a theological discussion but more a practical working out, I feel we need just to explain briefly that God has to allow this sinful world to suffer the consequences of its sinful nature, and we are all part of this world. The other side of the coin is that God offers grace to those who suffer, and help in time of need. It's good also to point out that when the final judgement comes, abusers and oppressors will get what they deserve (see 2 Pet 2:9).

Having lived in London, we are very much aware of our sin-sick society and the huge amount of emotional damage that surrounds us. And if we in the church are not set free, how can we help the world outside?

Let us look at some of the possible reasons for emotional damage. The list we are giving you consists mainly of those things that have affected us in our lives, so we know about them!

Firstly, severe shock or trauma can have a lasting effect on us emotionally. We mentioned in the previous chapter about the death of our son, only a year old, which was a severe shock. It caused great heartache and trauma, which damaged us emotionally. Even if you know the person is going to die, there is still emotional trauma when you lose somebody you love, especially when you have been with them for many years.

We can also be damaged by divorce, and although we have not experienced that ourselves we have counselled many who have experienced divorce and the trauma that it causes.

Moving house can also cause a lot of emotional damage and this is something we have experienced many times! When your husband is a minister and he resigns, you have to move. Your house is part of the job so you lose everything in one go. You have to start again and it is very hard. You are separated from friends, and your children also suffer emotional damage as they have to leave schools and lose friends and security.

If you have a husband who has to move through promotion or perhaps through redundancy you will appreciate what we are saying. Redundancy itself and unemployment in this day and age are other factors that will cause emotional hurt. Another major cause which, added to any other factor, causes devastating effects is being unloved or rejected. There are hundreds of teenagers in London alone who are homeless because of rejection or lack of love. Abuse, both verbal and physical, is another reason for being without home and security and being in need of healing. Praise God there is healing in Jesus.

Hopefully, as we share testimonies and cases where healing has taken place, you will be able to receive healing yourself. God is the only answer to this sin-sick world. We want you to be able to stand complete in him and deal with your problems and cope with your emotions. You can then minister to those in need.

In Chapter 1 we wrote about the enemy's arrows. The enemy will lose no time in directing them at damaged or impaired emotions. He has a strategy to kill, steal and destroy, and he is a liar and a thief. He will attack our weak points. Wherever he can get in he will (see Jn 8:44; 10:10). Some of the enemy arrows that attack us can cause continual sickness–an arrow of infirmity which attacks the body. This may seem strange to you, but we know of someone who was continually being sick and had many operations. After being prayed for and her emotional damage being healed, she was set free and her health slowly improved.

One that attacks the mind is an arrow of false guilt or over-responsibility. This leads to trying to please, which we mentioned in connection with shame and humiliation. We can wear ourselves out trying to please people. Others in the church can actually manipulate and control us and we can have this terrible burden of trying to fulfill every-one's desires. We are no good to God while we are attacked like this. God wants us to learn how to hear him and do his will.

Fears of all kinds are enemy arrows: fears of death, sickness, fears of the enemy himself. It's like a continual cycle of events leading to damaged emotions, and yet fears are rooted in damaged emotions and so you find you are going round in circles.

So we come to what we want to deal with mainly in this chapter, and that is the fact that damaged emotions lead to sexual problems. We have a weakness and therefore give in to sexual sins.

We have tried to put these sexual problems in the order in which they affect us, starting with those that affect the mind. The thought-life is linked with the emotions. Sexual problems begin in the thought-life and end in the body. In fact nearly all our problems start in the thought-life. How important it is that we use the helmet of salvation to keep our minds in purity of thought, kept by the power of Jesus throught the Holy Spirit.

When our mind dwells on something fearful, unless we confront the fear our minds will go out of control and we will be tormented. We need to protect our minds. It's not wrong to be tempted; what is wrong is giving in to the temptation.

Although this chapter will be concerned with case studies and testimonies, plus a biblical method for being set free, nevertheless we need to look at some passages and problems to set the scene.

First, as an encouragement, here are some Scripture passages of comfort. Romans 8:1–2 states that 'there is now no condemnation for those who are in Christ Jesus'. He has set us free from sin.

Colossians 3:10 tells of a new creation and the old being put to death. We need to note that our body is the temple of the Holy Spirit. These scriptures are not giving us the freedom to sin. In the past few years many have though they are free to sin because Jesus will forgive and set them free again and again. This is not what the words mean. It is not all right to sin continually. The enemy will get in and cause havoc in your life if you adopt this attitude. Our freedom is that we are free to say 'no' to sin–not to succumb but to say 'no'–because if Jesus Christ is the same yesterday, today and for ever then we conclude that God has not changed his standards. We do not change God's standards. We need to come to the throne with clean hands and a pure heart. What we want to see is revival in our churches, but we will not get revival unless we are willing to make our bodies the temple of the Holy Spirit. The Lord wants to use us to show an example to the world, but if we are portraying a sin-sick church we are not attracting people to Jesus.

The first sexual problem that we need to deal with is self-idolatry, or loving oneself, which leads to masturbation. We will set the scene with Scripture and look at Exodus 20: 'I am the Lord your God, who brought you out of Egypt, out of the land of slavery. You shall have no other gods before me. You shall not make for yourself an idol in the form of anything in heaven above or on the earth beneath or in the waters below' (vv. 2–4).

'But mark this: There will be terrible times in the last days'–that is not unfamiliar, is it?–for 'people will be lovers of themselves, lovers of money, boastful, proud, abusive . . . ungrateful, unholy . . . having a form of godliness' (2 Tim 3:1–2,5).

If you love yourself–and we are not talking here about loving your neighbour as yourself but about yourself being the whole centre of your universe to the exclusion of God– then you become the substitute to the place that God should fill. Self-idolatry is loving oneself to the exclusion of God in the area of one's weakness.

This is a substitute and I was challenged myself on this just over a year ago in one little area. I was being counselled. If you are a counsellor, it's important that you too are open to being counselled. I just made a chance remark that made the cousellor pounce! In this particular area I was excluding the Lord. It was not the area that we are dealing with here, but what they were saying was that I was excluding the Lord in a part of my life, although I was baptised in the Spirit, baptised in water, a Bible-believing Christian, fully paid up church member, pastor, whatever! In this area I had not noticed that I had broken the first commandment and I repented of it and I was forgiven.

We have to be so careful. There are so many distractions that we could make an idol where God has nothing to do with that area of life whatsoever. It therefore is quite far reaching.

Now what I am going to share here you may not agree with, but please give me a fair hearing by reading through and then praying about it with an open mind. Read what the Bible says and get before God and ask his Spirit to reveal to you the truth about yourself. There are some counsellors who do not follow the path that we do—not many, but there are some.

I want to make some comments so you know where I am coming from. Wet dreams and the bodily changes of adolescence belong to the child and not to the adult. We are not talking here about the growing-up process and pains of adolescence where sometimes their bodily functions are beyond their control. This is part of growing up and we are not talking about that part of our development. What we are talking about is that if we are an adult in Christ there comes a time when we can say like Paul in 1 Corinthians 13:11, 'When I was a child, I talked like a child, I thought like a child, I reasoned like a child. When I became a man, I put childish ways behind me.' Adolescence belongs to the development of our childhood and makes way for adulthood, and at some point in our adulthood we should put childish things away. When these tendencies are not put away, then they become deliberate and that is the point we are writing about.

Deliberate masturbation is a sign of loving one's self for satisfaction or substitute love. We have lost count of the people we have counselled in the area–committed Christians who in adulthood have a weakness in this way.

This breaks the first commandment, for we love ourselves rather than God in this area. It can become self-idolatry, regardless of the motive behind it. It is not really the act of clean hands and a pure heart since it is a perversion of what is right and proper between a man and a woman.

It would help if at this point we shared with you the story of a woman who sought help in this problem, who has given permission for us to share and whose name we will call June.

As a small child June had a lot of sickness in her life, and despite the love and care of Christian parents she had to spend a lot of time alone and remembers that masturabation started in the cot as a toddler. She also recalls that as she grew older the problem became worse as it was associated with sexual fantasies. This worried her a great deal as the fantasies were things that a child would not think of, so why had she all these terrible thoughts? In her teens the situation was no better and although she hoped the problem would go away, in fact it did not. Added to the problem now was shame, humiliation, guilt and a fear that so gripped her that she dared not seek help. It seemed to her that the Christians around her would be totally horrified if she dared open up, and might reject her completely. She prayed hard for release and yet was locked up, totally unable to speak about it. As she became a committed Christian she managed to control the problem better, but whenever she was depressed or hurt it would rear its ugly head, and again she was locked into guilt and shame.

She also realised that this was more than a habit and that somehow the enemy was using her weakness to gain entry into her thought-life. She prayed harder for the help she most needed–someone in whom she could confide. She began to pray for such a person whom she knew and respected who might understand. She wanted to go on with God and this was a stumbling-block in the way. After a healing conference she found someone in whom she could confide and all the years of pain and hurt came gushing in tears of release.

A great deal of healing was done just by sharing and confessing her need and also in realising that she was not the great sinner that she thought she was, but that others too suffered in this way, and it was a way of loving herself because of the loneliness all those years ago. Satan had then taken advantage of the little girl as only he would and enemy arrows had infiltrated her mind, bringing unclean and lustful thoughts that were obviously not her own.

So began the healing first of the emotions, with the repenting of the sin, renouncing the enemy and beginning the physical healing which would release June of the habit. A habit like this will take time to break, but at least the end was in view after years and years of being locked up in suffering and shame. Her first reaction was: Why are Christians so closed when it comes to problems like this? Why do we allow others to think we do not suffer in this way, hence making a gap between us and allowing the enemy to have a victory?

Hence the reason we are being so open in this chapter. There are many more who need to know that Christians have emotions that are exploited by the enemy and the result is self-idolatry in that area alone where God has no part. Nor can he desire a part, for he cannot look upon the sin that develops in the fantasy world.

If you read your Bible you will notice that stress is made right through the Bible on purity. Our body is the temple of the Holy Spirit and masturbation is a weakness that can be exploited by the enemy. It is not the way of self-control. One of the functions of the Holy Spirit is to come upon a person and produce love, joy, peace and also self-control. If you think about it, we are not dealing here with an act of self-control but a problem of no self-control. If we look at Jesus, it is unthinkable that in all his purity and holiness he could countenance such an act involving impurity.

The problem is that unless the habit is broken and the cause behind it healed, it becomes the base for other sexual sins. We know this to be true from all those we have counselled in this way. We can pray for release, but the hardest part is then breaking the habit which has built up over a long time and replacing the habit with clean and pure acts. The healing is easy; deliverance is relatively easy, but breaking a habit is not so straight-forward. We sow a thought, we reap an act; we sow an act, we reap a habit; we sow a habit, we reap a character. Some psychologists will say that it takes eighteen months to break a habit, but I want to say that Jesus can do things much quicker, and even overnight if we co-operate with him!

Let me tell you about two other people. One I have named Gemma and the other Grace. Both want others to know their testimony so that perhaps another person can be helped.

Gemma is a lovely Christian lady. When she was born she was very ill and almost died. The first two or three years of her life were spent in bed. She was not neglected, but had to spend hours alone. When praying for her, it became clear that this is where the root of her masturbation started–through isolation. So started many, many years of a sexual problem which resulted, like June, in a habit, sexual fantasies, guilt and shame. There was no one to talk to. It was never mentioned in Christian circles and she just felt that if they had known, it would mean condemnation and that was not what she needed! She lived a life of guilt. Over the years she had this intense desire to be free and at long last, through much prayer, she found help. We were able to show her that she was not the only one. The times people have said to us: 'I don't know how to tell you because there cannot be anyone as bad as me', and you could cry for them because you know that there are lots of Christians who have never sought help, and here is one desiring to be more like Jesus, pure and holy. Slowly we prayed for her and saw her completely set free as she confessed the sin behind masturbation in adulthood and walked free from the pain and the pressure.

Grace is a teenager. She too loved herself and suffered with sexual problems. She came from a Christian home, but her father did not speak to her much. There was little communication in the home. Her mother gave her very little love that was physical—few kisses and hugs. In fact there was more judgemental communication than love. Between the two of them they had not given Grace a good pattern for life. When she came to her teenage years she began to feel the guilt and the shame. Yet who could she turn to? She met with Christians, but they did not talk about such things. No one seemed to be on her wavelength. It wasn't the sort of thing that anyone mentioned, until she met a friend at school who was older than she was and appeared to have all the answers.

This girl admitted a similar pattern in her own life and said to her, 'What you need is love—the love that I can give you. It's harmless, you won't get pregnant and your needs will be fulfilled'.

Grace found herself swept along with this dominant friend into a lesbian relationship. If only the Christians had not been so silent, would the relationship still have developed? That girl is not free today. She walked out of our home, unwilling to forgive those who had ignored her all those years. As a teenager she did not feel she had the opportunity to share her need. There are many more young people on the streets in similar situations and they need our love and our care and our support, not our condemnation.

I want to share more fully about the link between masturbation and sexual fantasies. As a counsellor my experience has been that most of those who have had this problem have sensed a power of overwhelming feelings and intense desire, which results in lust. This is exploited by enemy arrows. This can happen at any time but more often when one is lonely. In counselling we have found that there is nearly always a fantasy element present and an enjoyment of the experience at the time, followed by regret, remorse and guilt, often with shame and loathing of oneself afterwards. A deep sense of guilt leads to the question: Why can't I help myself? This is often accompanied by the resolve in remorse that it will never happen again, which only deepens the guilt and shame next time. There is neither the power nor the strength to break the pattern and nearly always there is the consciousness that this is not a godly thing.

Out of all the countless number of people we have counselled, this is a typical pattern: the temptation, the enjoyment of the experience at the time the act was committed, followed by intense remorse over what has occurred, followed by guilt and loathing and a resolve to do better next time, only in most cases to find that the pattern is repeated, ending up with failure being built in.

Now I want to declare that Jesus Christ can not only heal the wounds that caused the self-love, but can forgive the sin and give strength to break the habit. We need to declare that Jesus Christ is able to deliver us from all sin and that the blood of Jesus cleanses us from all sin because he is God. The only way we will ever be free is to allow the Spirit of God to bring us his release.

Psalm 24:3 says, 'Who may ascend the hill of the Lord? Who may stand in his holy place? He who has clean hands and a pure heart.' That is our aim: that we present people before God with clean hands and a pure heart.

Just a short note now on sexual fantasies. These are not uncommon, especially where there has been a stern upbringing or a lonely life. The feeling of being involved is associated with this as well, and therefore single people are vulnerable.

The following are contributory factors in this. Reading immoral romantic books. They usually have a heroine and a hero, and the story line is very puerile. To all intents and purposes it represents what we would like to see happening in our lives, but usually in such plots they land up in bed, and that is immoral. We see it on TV, in films and in literature, and yet it is against God's law for man. It is wrong. The peer pressure of the world is: if you like someone, then there is no harm in it. But this is not what God intended for his people, and God cannot look upon sin.

For those who are lonely and have no partner in life, the temptation is to fantasise what might occur and we have counselled those who have done just this and suffered shame, humiliation and guilt. Some have shared how they have fantasised themselves into the story book and lived in unreality, which led to masturbation and had a complete stronghold over them for years and years. Throught-life must be checked. I know we all indulge in day-dreams and this is not what we are talking about. I had day-dreams. I dreamed that one day I would fall in love with this fantastic girl and how she would take care of me! Yes, I dreamed of such things, but I also brought them to God, who pruned my fantasies so that I began to pray and ask God what sort of girl I should marry; and in my prayers I began to receive revelation about her which was to be fulfilled. First, her name would be Jean! She would be a nurse and she would be a keen Christian with a missionary interest in the places where I had a missionary interest. Fourthly, when we met, she would be going on the same holiday as me in the summer and we would both know in a very short space of time that we were right for one another.

God honoured that prayer. It took two years to come to fruition and that's another story. When I met Jean all those prayer conditions were met! I proposed after just four hours because we saw God's hand in everything we shared. Needless to say this is a very rare, true romance!

I had allowed God to prune my fantasies, and my prayers became reality. Twenty-nine years of faithfulness in marriage is something to thank God for. It cannot be bad, can it?

If we do not bring our thought-life to the foot of the cross and allow God to inspect our thoughts, and the word of God and the Spirit of God to work in us, we are in big trouble. Fantasy leads us into unreality, which in turn takes us into the kingdom of darkness.

The next sin we are going to look at in the area of sexual sins is coveting. There is quite a lot in the Bible about coveting. In the Ten Commandments it says very clearly: 'You shall not covet your neighbour's house. You shall not covet your neighbour's wife, or his manservant or his maidservant, his ox or donkey, or anything that belongs to your neighbour' (Exod 20:17). Paul the apostle, when he wrote in Romans about sin entrapping him, found there was one little item called coveting that had ensnared him. He doesn't say what he coveted, so we are not going to lay any possibilities as to what it might or might not have been, but he admits that he coveted.

In the Old Testament, if you read Joshua 7:1–26, you find the sin of Achan who, when they destroyed the city, coveted raiment and gold and silver, and buried them. God punished the whole people, so God obviously sees coveting as serious.

Coveting is mentioned in Corinthians and Galatians. It is a lust, whether it be weak or powerful. Strong coveting means you cannot keep your hands off someone's property and usually ends in stealing. It's a desire to have something that has not been given to you and to lust after it until it is yours. It is in effect the 'I want' syndrome and the most powerful case in the whole of the Bible is found in Isaiah 14: Satan's fall.

If you get consumed by lust in the sexual realm, then it will consume you with overwhelming feelings and have all sorts of repercussions. You can covet the girl down the road who is married. A husband can covet another friend's wife. The enemy is a thief and a destroyer and if you have someone's wife then you have destroyed a relationship and stolen someone who belonged to someone else. You have in effect killed a relationship. This will affect your relationship with God, which will also be in danger of being destroyed. We can see therefore how coveting another brings brokenness, destruction and murder.

My English master at school had quite a fiery temper. He was always letting off steam and you could see the colour rise in his face as his anger rose. Basically his heart was right and he used to come out with some gems. If my memory of forty years serves me right, this is what he said: 'If you are capable of sexual sins you are more than capable of murder'. Now that may seem strong, but there is a lot in what he actually said. When we get into the realm of adultery and fornication, it is destruction of a relationship and then it's possible to go one step further. Many times on the news in recent days we have actually heard of cases where this has happened and a wife or a boyfriend has been murdered. Therefore what we are talking about is serious.

We ought to say a few words about fornication. In the world today there is so much peer pressure. It's in our schools and our universities. We had a Christian brother whose daughter had to leave the university because she was too upset by the sexual behaviour of the rest of the girls in the block where she was living. The peer pressure is everywhere—in the streets and at work—and not just peer pressure but pressure to be one of the crowd, not to be the odd one out. There is so much in this present world which as alien to the standards of the gospel.

God does not change his standards. Jesus said in Mark 7:21, 'Out of men's hearts come evil thoughts . . . murder, adultery . . .'. It starts in the thought-life. Your brain tells you what you need to do. It all begins in the mind, which is pressurised by external forces (see Rom 1:18–32). There has been so much in the headlines of Christian newspapers about the conditions of immorality in this present country alone.

First Corinthians 6 is a relevant and helpful chapter to read, but also in the Old Testament fornicators were either put to death to maintain the purity of God's people, or they were forced to marry the victim. That was the only alternative. We live in the New Testament era, where we still press for purity, but those who fall into sin sexually are not dealt with as if under the old law, for example, with a death penalty. We do not condone the sin, but we do try to love the sinner and show them the grace of God, whereby they can be forgiven and change their ways.

If we are going to be a witness to the world, we have to show that God can change such people. Then we can offer an alternative lifestyle. We can say that Jesus has set them free and given them a life which is far more beautiful and more fulfilled. Christ has met their needs, for the cross is all-sufficient. Sex before marriage is forbidden by the Scriptures, but sometimes we have to face the reality that it does happen and we must not shirk our responsibilities in this. I have pastored those who have let God down in this way and they have not been repentant. I have had to put them out of fellowship because they were not a good example to follow. You would think that in a small place that would cause all sorts of reactions. I walked along the road one afternoon and a non-Christian got hold of me and said, 'I want a word with you! I want to say I admire you for making a stand in what you did.' Now we had not deliberately broadcast the fact, but it had come to her notice and she said, 'In this day and age when the church is so weak on issues, I am so pleased there are some people in the church strong enough to do the right thing'. Now we did give these folk pastoral care so that we could have a report back if there was a change. Putting out of fellowship is not the end. The end is to seek to restore that vital relationship with God.

That word of encouragement from a non-Christian made me feel so relieved because when you are the one who has to stick your neck out, you also carry the can! Here is the experience of a Christian brother.

'I am a sinful man, but it is my joy today that Christ came not for the righteous but for sinners to repent. In 1986 I became a Christian. I felt I had everything. In fact I spoke to myself when I was walking alone and said, 'I have got everything I need'. I was on fire and jumped for joy. I remember going on a retreat during the week following my exams, and the joy of the Lord was over-whelming within me. I thought I could cope with every-thing, but Satan actually played on my weak area, which actually I did not realise.

'A week later I was involved in a sexual relationship which led to a child being born. I knew that what I had got myself involved in was not right. You may ask why I did it. I can only answer that I did it and I lost the joy, lost the desire to read God's word, I lost the desire to pray and, worst of all, none of my Christian friends knew of the relationship or of the child. I was reduced to a one-day church-goer, just Sunday morning. Each time I went to church I would end up crying within me that I was not right with God. One thing was keeping me going and that was a promise from God: "If we confess our sin he is faithful and just and will forgive us our sin and cleanse us from unrighteousness." I marked that in my Bible and knew it included my sexual sin that I was deep into at that time. I concealed everything from all my friends, and all they knew was that I was a Christian. I would go to one place and I was respected as a Christian, but deep within me

I knew I was not right with God, and eventually I decided I must open up and tell the truth. It was not an easy thing to do, to expose myself–especially in this area, but I knew I had to do it. I told a friend that I had committed a sexual sin and that I had a child and no one knew. I said I needed to be prayed for, and this friend of mine prayed for me.

'Afterwards I had a tremendous relief; a relief from having told someone, and then I told another friend who also prayed for me. One day I decided to bring my daughter to my present church and this was a surprise to my care group and the church members. I battled with myself. "What am I going to tell them–that this is my niece?" Then someone came straight out with it–"That looks like your daughter". "Yes, she is mine. She is my daughter." That was another great relief. I was then able to say to others. "Meet my daughter".

I thank God that I now have the joy of the Lord within me, having been prayed for and sought forgiveness. I enjoy reading the Bible again. I have prayed on several occasions and received an answer, which has assured me of God's forgiveness which I was longing for. When I read my Bible I read what David wrote: "How happy are those whose sins are forgiven. Their transgressions are covered up." I was so glad. Amen!'

When you have been through a time of sexual sin, however much you feel forgiven there will be a scar on the memory that may take time to heal. We have prayed with those who have borne scars for twenty or even thirty years because they have left such a deep mark. We want to bless our brother for sharing his heart with us and pray that it may encourage many others to seek forgiveness at the cross of Jesus. We are not making excuses for those who fall into sin, but the pressure in the world in which we live today is very powerful and we need to be aware of that fact. We need to understand why they do what they do.

One of the reasons for falling into sexual sin is the need to be loved. In the past their parents did not demonstrate love and rejected them. The sad thing is to have parents who loved you but not in the way that you want. Rejection still appears and rejection is the most common reason for a person to fall into sexual sin. The desire to be loved is very strong. The church needs to teach more on role models for parents. Marrying couples is not the end of the church's task; it should be the beginning.

The peer pressure today has badly affected our teen-agers. We need to understand them, not condemn them. We must pray for them and show them a better way.

At the root of all this is an inner need to be loved and accepted, and that is so basic to our deepest needs. That is why God is a God of love. He wants a relationship that touches our deepest and basic needs. It's not new clothes I need or a plateful of food or a roof over my head, although these are necessary, but deep down it's relationships.

This was shown very clearly on the news only recently when a young couple from war-torn Bosnia and Serbia tried to escape so that they could be together, leaving shelter and belongings, and died together in each other's arms. What I need most of all is to be loved and to be able to be loved without something or someone spoiling it. We have a great need to be loved. Many of these wrong relationships are spawned in the need to be loved.

Now we need to write about adultery, which is clearly forbidden, and at the end of the chapter you will find some texts to read up. Jesus said that you can lust after a person in your mind and that is the same as adultery. Lust can be equated with coveting. You can look upon a person and desire them and commit emotional adultery.

Pastors have wonderful privileges, but sometimes God gives strong words of warning, and as pastors we have to give these warnings and give heed to them, despite the consequences.

Adultery is stealing a partner who belongs in a covenant relationship. This is probably for Christians the most serious of all. When we are married we are in a covenant relationship with God: 'Let no man put asunder what God has joined together'. We need to make divorce more difficult, not easier, especially where Christians are concerned. We need to have greater pastoral care over the problems to resolve them.

We need to pass on quickly before closing this chapter and mention the homosexual and lesbian relationships, which are clearly forbidden by Scripture, and at the end of the chapter you will find references to look up.

Sexual deviation is an offence to God. It is found both in the Old Testament and the New. What saddens me is Christians who claim to be 'gay'. They need deliverance and counselling, for they have been sadly led astray. Any marriage performed by the church between the same sex is an abomination to God. I have had to counsel people like this and have felt sick inside, although I have never let my own feelings stand in the way of them being set free in Christ's forgiving love. God is able to set these folk free and we can witness to this.

Very often the common cause is rejection, especially by Mum or Dad or by both parents, or not being loved in the correct way. Physical abuse, verbal abuse and sexual abuse are nearly always present. There is nearly always a contributory factor. Sometimes there is a spiritual reason, when a curse has been handed down the family. In my experience that is not so common as the other causes. Emotional damage leads to lustful thought-life, which will be a strong foothold for ungodly practices. Once you are into these practices, then you receive further emotional damage and a cycle of events takes place that is impossible to get out of. Jesus is the only answer–a recognition of the sin involved bringing about a true repentance.

We need to make a clear stand against homosexuality and lesbianism, but also make it clear that we want to help the person to be released and recognise the events of life which have trapped them in this way. We love the sinner and hate the sin.

There are other sexual perversions which we need to mention, as the Bible prohibits them, and I have given you the Scriptures for them at the end of the chapter.

Although the following is not common, it does happen. I have counselled a person who, because he was unloved and unwanted, turned to his pet for love, which became perverted. Most folk never get anywhere near this type of sexual sin, but it does happen and deep down there is the sense of shame. As he confessed and renounced his sin, God set him free.

The reason God circumcised the Israelites on the eighth day was to show that he was the master of their bodies from the earliest of days. Because all the other heathen nations around them were into sexual perversions, God gave the Israelites a set of commands so they would be different from the rest of the world. God has not changed his mind. He wants a people today who through the blood of Jesus are made pure, and a holy people who will walk in purity.

Scripture to study

Adultery: Matthew   5:27–28
  Romans   1:18–32
  1 Corinthians   5:9–12
  1 Corinthians   6:12–20

Homosexuality and lesbianism:
  Genesis   19:4–8
  Leviticus   18:22; 20:13
  Judges   19:22–24
  Romans   1:18–32
  1 Thessalonians   4:3–8

Sexual perversions:
  Exodus   22:19
  Leviticus   18:6–30; 20:15–16

At this stage we are giving you a pattern to follow to help free yourself if any of the previous chapters apply to you. This pattern will help you in any of the problems that you find as you read and seek the help of the Holy Spirit to convict you of any sin in your own life. This biblical pattern will also help you to help others.

1. Confess the sin to God (with a trusted friend if this helps) and repent of the sin you are in.
2. Forgive anyone involved (including yourself).
3. Renounce the sin: 'I will no longer allow . . . to have a hold over me'.
4. Receive the healing of Jesus. (Here it will help to have a trusted friend or leader in your church who understands to pray with you, but if this is not possible ask Jesus to fill you with his healing love and power).
5. Learn to use your armour (Chapter 1) The Scriptures we have mentioned will help you.

Renew your mind in his work (Rom 12:1–3), trusting the Holy Spirit to keep you and fill you with the power of Jesus. Find those you can trust to pray with you when you feel weak.

The Lord wants to bring us to a place of freedom and a place of peace with himself. He genuinely desires our best, but sexual breaches of his laws bring upon ourselves the curse of his disapproval. In the Old Testament this carried on to the third and fourth generations, but Christ died to redeem us from the curse. Let us reverse the curse through the cross of Christ Jesus. The blood of Christ Jesus cleanses us from all sin.

Many diseases today can be traced back to sexual sins. The Scripture says we will reap what we sow. Therefore let us sow to the glory of God and reap accordingly.

4

Relationships: Church and God

Did you know that Jesus is praying for you today? Did you know that he intercedes at the right hand of God the Father for you? This is the heart of his prayer:

> My prayer is not for them alone. I pray also for those who will believe in me through their message, that all of them may be one, Father, just as you are in me and I am in you. May they also be in us so that the world may believe that you have sent me. I have given them the glory that you gave me, that they may be one as we are one: I in them and you in me. May they be brought to complete unity to let the world know that you sent me and have loved them even as you have loved me (Jn 17:20–23).

So Jesus' heart today is that we become one. We can only be one as we begin to understand one another. Oneness does not mean cloning so that we are all the same! He made us all to be individuals, and in this chapter we want to share a little about how we can understand one another. He wants us to learn to love and care for one another.

Let us look at relationships in relation to us as an army of God's people. Soldiers do not stand alone. They need one another. An army is not made up of individuals fighting alone, but of people who fight together. Our one aim should be to put down the enemy. Is that our aim today, or are we too busy fighting each other? What is our aim?

Jesus prayed that we would have the victory over the
enemy. If the enemy can fire enough arrows to break up
our relationships he will. His aim is to destroy the church,
so we are prime targets (Jn 10:10a; 1 Pet 5:8). Often
because Christians do not realise who it is that is attacking, they blame one another, hence division results and the
arrow has succeeded in its mission. There is no greater
time than today for the enemy to try and break up the
church. There are more divisions in the Christian church
than there have ever been before. We have an enemy who
knows his time is running out and if he can break us up he
will. Jesus is saying to us today that we need to be one, not
that we need to meet in one church, but that we are united
against the enemy attack. Those of us who know and love
the Lord Jesus are one in spirit. We should therefore be
loving one another, not condemning and criticising. We
need to support one another, not hurt.

If your brother or sister has hurt you, see where he or
she is coming from, because behind that remark is an
enemy arrow and very often we are not aware of it and
neither is the person who has hurt us. If we start to see
behind the remark and see what the enemy is trying to
do, then we will have an understanding that will help us
to accept people as they are and fight the spirit that has
been sent to destroy. The gossip, the lies, the evil
thoughts are all enemy arrows to destroy Christian
relationships.

Ephesians 4:32 says: 'Be kind and compassinate to one
another, forgiving each other, just as in Christ God forgave you.' That is the plea that the Lord Jesus would come
to us with.

Relationships begin in the thought-life. In every chapter
we come back to the thought-life and begin to realise how
important the helmet of salvation is to us. Sift your
thought-life about one another. Where are the thoughts
coming from? God or the enemy or your own selfish
ambitions? Ask yourself whether God says these things

to you: 'He dislikes you'; 'They are talking about you'. Does God say, 'You are a failure'?

We know that God does not say these things. They either come from an enemy arrow or from within ourselves. Start sifting your thoughts and hence prevent them developing into something you cannot cope with. The helmet of salvation is there to assist us in protecting our minds and guarding them from unwanted thoughts and hence needs to be worn. Whenever we feel attacked (and incidentally it isn't wrong to feel attacked–what is wrong is giving in!) if we are sitting at home or in church and the thought comes into our mind that what someone has said to us is unkind, we must claim the helmet of salvation to protect our mind and reject the thought. We mustn't dwell on it. We must deal with it, otherwise the arrow will take root in bitterness or anger or resentment.

Now let us think about how relationships come about. They are often built upon the pattern of our own upbringing. If we were encouraged and feel good about ourselves, then we will do the same for others. If we had a bad upbringing where we were criticised and not encouraged, then we will find relationships difficult. The wonderful thing is that the Lord can heal us so that we can enjoy relationships that are good and healthy.

Many who come into the church today have had a very difficult upbringing and we are seeing God heal these folk and give them a new attitude towards people whom they relate to: If the pattern of upbringing is one of broken home, abuse and continual stress, then we as Christians will need to understand where they are coming from so that our understanding of them in relating to us is good. Then we can help others. If we were encouraged at home to feel good about ourselves, then we will do the same for others. If as Christians we did not have that type of upbringing, then we are in danger of being critical and need to seek the Lord for healing so that we are able to relate to the wounded and distressed in the world. We can then ask the Lord to show us where they are hurting and pray for them without our own self getting in the way. God needs a whole army today more than ever before to deal with the wounded. We want to restore love to the world by showing the love of Jesus, because that is what he did. We need to understand the fears and the pride that enter relationships.

God does not want us to prove ourselves by trying to show we are always right. He wants us to show a better way, by love and example. Sometimes it's the fear of what others will think that causes us to have a bad attitude towards one another.

The Scripture talks a lot about one another and we are going to point out how these scriptures can help us in relationships. I feel somewhat qualified to write about the 'one another' because four years ago I made an intensive study on this. The 'one another' ministry is a ministry to each other. 'Love one another'–much easier said than done. After all, there are some very difficult folk–even in the church! Nevertheless, the Bible says 'Love one another.' It's a command!

'Accept one another!' This may appear easy on the outside, but inwardly sometimes we are groaning. What we appear on the outside, as we very well know, is not necessarily so on the inside. We might find it easier to 'admonish one another'! Is it easier to tell each other off? Remember if you do this, expect it to be done to you, and remember that the Bible does say 'in love'. Often that part is forgotten.

'Care for one another.' We all need to be loved and accepted and cared for, and would accept admonishing if first we were loved, accepted and cared for.

We also need to 'teach and submit to one another'. There are times when we submit to each other, even male to female! In our first pastorate, my wife would get a word from the Lord and suggest I needed to visit a certain person and I often ignored her suggestions, thinking, 'I am the boss here!' I found to my cost that I needed at times to listen to my wife because on several occasions the ones she had suggested I visit died before I reached them. I have learned that sometimes even the most humble or insignificant brother or sister may have a word that we need to heed. It's not that we don't sift it or weigh it—we can still do that—but in a 'one another' ministry we all have a part and God has a ministry to us through each other. Ask the Lord which one you need to practise out of these 'one another' ministries. When you have time alone with God have a close look at the 'one another' ministries and see which ones you can effectively practise in your own life. It is very true in the Christian life that if you do not practise you cannot become perfect! We belong to a practical faith.

Let us now look at our relationship with God. The model prayer that Jesus taught his disciples was: when you pray, pray like this, 'Our Father.. . . . ' Relationship with God is like one of a child to his father. You need to become a child of God through faith in the Lord Jesus Christ:. 'Yet to all who received him, to those who believed in his name, he gave the right to become children of God' (Jn 1:12).

Our relationship with God is like that of a Father. We have received the Spirit whereby we can cry, 'Abba Father.' God has blessed us with every spiritual blessing in the heavenly places (Eph 1; Rom 8; see also 1 Jn 3:1–2).

How do we see God? of course you will see God as Father in the Bible, but deep in your heart how do you see God? Your feelings may not necessarily see God as the Bible sees him. The answer to this affects all our relationships.

Do you see God with a whip in his hand or a tear in his eye? Is he like an Egyptian task-master to you, with a whip waiting to knock you down at the least sign of faltering so that you work, work, work, then perhaps at the end of the day hope you have won approval or some respite? Or do you see him as the Father of the prodigal son, such that whenever you appear he runs with arms open wide and puts his arms about you and welcomes you with tears in his eyes?

This last way is not the way a typical father behaves in the east, but it is the way that God behaves towards us. He comes to meet us with tears and love in his eyes.

I have a Christian brother who, though we may not always agree on everything, has a most anointed ministry in the realm of emotional healing, and as I worked with him I learned a lot from him and we are brothers together. We were once in a meeting together, ministering together about emotional healing. He asked the men to close their eyes and relax and allow the Spirit of God to fall on them. He then said he was going to mention one word to us, and while we were relaxed with our defences down this word would drop into our subconscious and we would rise with an answer.

The word he said was 'father'. This word dropped like a great rock into a still pool and I came to with a sudden start as I saw this big stick in a hand, and I knew that was how I saw Father God. I thought, 'Why is this?' and I relaised that was how I saw my earthly father, who was a small man and a schoolmaster. Not only that, he was my schoolmaster. So to make sure I had no favouritism, he often came down heavy on me. Out would come the stick at any suspicion of me being the culprit. It must not be seen that father had favourites. Now I knew my father loved me, but the way I saw it and the way it coloured my life also coloured my perceptions of God, and I saw him for many years as a rather stern and forbidding figure, such that if I did not toe the line, out would come the stick! I must behave myself and work hard a being a good Christian, otherwise he is waiting to pounce on me!

I have tried to put it in a lighter way, but there is a great deal of truth behind what I am saying for all of us. Many see God their Father as they do their earthly father and that perception has stood in the way of freeedom to relate to

God in the correct way. Our childhood plays an important part in how we see our heavenly Father. Do we see him with whip in hand or a tear in his eye?

The Bible says that God does discipline those he loves, but he does so in love. Over the years my biblical view of God has altered so that I now see God as a Father who wants the best for me and loves me enough to discipline in a loving way (Heb 12:5–11; Prov 3:11–12). In other words, how I see him is more in line with what he is.

Our heavenly Father delights in us (Jn 1:12; Rom 8:15) and really does love us. That is why he made us his children and blessed us with every spiritual blessing in heavenly places. Is your view of Father so stern that you do not enjoy all the blessings? I have to say that often I fall short of the blessings because I have an enemy who wants to steal and rob and destroy what God has given me. Nevertheless, in principle we have all the blessings and what we have to do is learn to enjoy them in practice, and that is one of the reasons why we are writing this book on setting the prisoner free.

Our relationship with God is more important than our position or office or ministry or what we can achieve. He did not die for your ministry or the works you could do. He did not die for all the good thoughts you could have about him or for the songs you could sing and the nice words you could say! He died for *you*. As you are. We can have as much of God as we want. How much of God *do* we want? I would like to think your spirit is like a balloon that has no limit to its expansion so you could have as much of God as you want.

When I was at college some thirty years ago, one of the students told of a boy who loved golden syrup and dreamed of a sea made of golden syrup, and in his dream he prayed, 'Lord, give me the capacity equal to my opportunity.' We have the opportunity to have as much of God as we want. Let the Lord give us the capacity equal to our opportunity. Some will receive more of God

because they seek more. Some will respond more because
they believe that he actually does love them. Others will
be rather tentative in their approach because they are not
too sure whether they are going to receive a whack or a
pat! I learned very early on that if the word 'Chris' was
called it was probably OK, but whenever I heard 'Chris-
topher' I had better start hiding because it meant trouble.

If we are open to God, then we will be open to one
another. Have you noticed that those who are really open
to God are the ones who will accept others? We need to
grasp what God is saying to us here, and if our pattern of
upbringing is affecting our relationship with God, then it
also affects our relationships with others and vice versa, so
we need to be set free.

If we ask the Holy Spirit, he will guide us in our
relationships. That is good. If I know the Holy Spirit is
guiding my relationships, then since the Spirit of God is
one of love and gentleness, if I let him choose my friends I
might receive some love and gentleness from my relationships! God will be working for my good.

If at the end of this chapter you feel you need help with
the pattern of your childhood, then first follow through the
pattern of being set free:

1. Confess any sin involved, e.g. wrong feelings
   towards Dad.
2. Forgive anyone involved (in this case your father).
3. Renounce the sin: 'I will no longer allow . . . to have
   a hold over me' (anger, resentment, etc.).
4. Receive the healing of Jesus–through a friend who
   can understand or a leader at your church whom you
   trust.

5

Christian Relationships

Let us look first at our relationships with other Christians.
These we should love as our own family (Jn 13:34–35; 1
Cor 13). I am assuming that you would naturally love your
own family! I firmly believe that is right. When our little
son died at the age of one year, that was a crushing blow to
me as I really loved him. I would have gladly put myself
in his place because I loved him so much and wanted to
spare him the pain and the suffering. It is that sort of
sacrificial love that we need in the Christian family–that
we love others as we love our family, for we would then
spare them the pain if we could, or better still bear it for
them. In our hearts we know it is true that when we love
someone we will suffer with them, and if we really love
them we will spare them every suffering it is possible to
spare. Following on from this is the command to forgive
one another: 'Be kind and compassionate to one another,
forgiving each other; just as Christ God forgave you' (Eph
4:32).

If you have a relationship with your fellow Christian
and yet have not forgiven them for something, then the
relationship causes hurt, and healing cannot take place.
You are always conscious of an obstacle or an obstruct-
ion between you. If I upset my husband and he upsets me
and it is unresolved or unforgiven I cannot rest. The
relationship is spoiled until we forgive and put ourselves
right before God, which we always do before the end of
the day.

I have found it is the same between a brother and sister in the church. If there is something that has happened and it has not been resolved or forgiven, I cannot settle or sleep, for it is like a thorn in the flesh. We need to take heed to the command to forgive because it is part of the father heart of God.

Another important fact in relationships in the church is to look at each other as equal in God's eyes. We are the same to God; we all have two eyes, two arms, one head, one body, two legs, are saved by one cross and we have one Saviour. There is one church, one baptism and we are all equal. Remembering this will save us from the danger of pride, so encourage one another (Heb 3:13).

I want to share here part of my own testimony concerning relationships in the Christian church. As a pastor's wife you may be surprised that I could have a two-year battle with Christian relationships, but that is what happened. Chris had resigned very suddenly from a church and when I say 'sudden' I mean that! It was completely a bolt out of the blue. One minute we were a happy, secure family unit and the next our world was upside down. We were uprooted and at that time I could not accept it. After all, our family of four would also be affected badly, with school work interrupted and friendships severed and to me it became too much. I therefore looked for someone to blame because isn't that what we very often do when things don't go our way? I blamed the church, the leaders and I blamed God. I suppose as I look back I could say I had a good reason to do that! The family was hurt and angry and upset. My mother had also moved to be near us and she too was upset as I had to break the news to her, and she too looked for someone to blame. All round it was an awful, total mess. Brothers and sisters, that is what happens when the enemy is allowed into a church and relationships are broken. We were on the receiving end. We are not saying we were not at fault, for as we look back we know none of us is perfect.

So in all this trauma and mess I decided that if there was a God he would have to show himself to me because I was not going near another church or Christians. I could not at that time trust a Christian for fear they would let me down. I sank myself back into my nursing and decided God would have to reveal himself to me. I did this even though he had wonderfully provided money for a home that would be ours. I found it impossible to forgive when I saw our children being turned away from Christians, which would have a lasting effect on them.

So I sank myself into what I could do best, my nursing, and said, 'Lord, if you really are there, then you will have to show me'. I love nursing and nursing means caring for people, and caring means relationships, even though they were not Christian relationships! Relationships is what I needed, because that is me. I am basically an open and loving person. Even if I take away the Christian belief, the pattern of loving and caring is still there. So as I loved people they began to open up to me and talk, and before long questions were being thrown at me that I could not avoid.

They asked me, 'Is there a God? Does God exist?' and it was non-Christians who brought me to my senses, because I realised here were people in need, people at the end of their lives, and if I did not tell them that the Lord Jesus was real, then I was failing in my duty! I could not go that far, so I started to share the gospel with one or two and led them to accept Jesus as their Lord. In doing that I found my faith again and forgave God, although at this point I had not forgiven Christians. You may find it quite amusing, but in my mind I thought I could happily lead these elderly people into the kingdom as they would then go straight to heaven, for there was no possibility of them going to church! This I thought was safe, for they would never suffer the problems of relating to other Christians. I thought I could carry on like this!

For two years I kept this up, until one day I realised that I needed to forgive my fellow brothers and sisters in Christ, and we booked up to go on another Wholeness Through Christ prayer ministry course. We had already been on one several years before and all this had happened since and I had felt too hurt to go on another course. When we did go, I had to get a group of people to pray for me that I would be able to share my heart without floods of tears. Not that tears were wrong, they were needful, but too many would mean I would be unable to verbalise what I wanted to say and to receive healing for the hurt and pain.

The wonderful thing about Wholeness Through Christ was the confidentiality, and meeting Christians I could trust. It was not so much that I was bitter but so desperately hurt and needed healing. It was only through my brothers and sisters praying for me that the pain began to go.

That battle is not always finished with, for whenever there are problems again, perhaps in the church, it can rear its ugly head and I have to learn to give things over to the Lord. God is healing me; he is teaching me not to hang on to hurt and pain and to learn to forgive. As I look back now I see that hanging on to hurt makes people feel sorry for you and we hang on because we have entered the 'poor old me's'. A lot of people would stand by me and say, 'You are right to feel like you do!' Yet that is not what relationships are all about. We need a Christ-like attitude in our lives of loving and forgiving.

There was only one person who never let me give in and that was Chris, my husband, and I can testify that I have never met a man so faithful to God. He quoted to me every single day, 'The God of all grace who called you to his eternal glory in Christ, after you have suffered a little while will himself restore and strengthen you and settle you'.

Chris made me quote that verse every day and I found that very hard, but I heard Chris shouting that verse around the house until he believed every part of it for himself and I knew that one day God would restore him, which he has!

Whenever we have problems in relationships with other Christians we are attacked by enemy arrows and I received a lot of them during my two-year battle to be set free. A word from someone who loves you does not hurt. There is no arrow behind it and that is so true—I can tell you that is true. We are happy for anyone to come and show us where they think we are wrong, as long as they have the love of Christ. If you are loved and cared for, you will receive a rebuke because the way it is given is for your good. If it is given like an enemy arrow, then the speaker will crush and wound and cause sleepless nights to the other person, until they forgive. That is true of all of us.

If you want a relationship that is open, then you have got to earn the right to speak into a person's life. We have no right to go to somebody and tell them they are wrong if we have never shown love to them. We cannot love them with word only—there must be deed as well. When we have had them in our home and shared a meal together and enjoyed each other's company, then we have a right to speak into their lives.

After eight years we had communication again with the church that hurt us so much, asking us to forgive them, and Chris had the joy of returning and preaching there. That is wonderful because it shows that God is in control, and if we leave it with him all things will work for our good. Praise God for that! Remember that where there are no enemy arrows you will not hurt your brother and sister, and you earn the right to speak only through love.

A word from Chris now about personality problems. Perhaps you think they do not exist in the church. The church is made up of all sorts. We have so many different varieties of people and sometimes people act more like a cheese grater and they rub us up the wrong way so we have personality clashes.

There are no easy ways to resolve these. The only way is to work through with God's grace and prayer. All things are possible to those who believe. I want to share here a personal testimony from my college days when I was doing my degree.

A student came to the college who had already got a first at Cambridge. I had studied metallurgy before going to do theology and as his first was in that area one would have thought we would get on well, but we did not! There didn't seem to be anything he did not know. There wasn't a thing he could not do. There wasn't an examination he could not pass and he had a very high opinion of himself, which gave me a complex! I had been brought up with the principle that you do not boast and you never speak about the things you can do unless you are asked, and then you say it and leave it, not boast about what you can do. This was like an anathema to me and every time I saw him I reacted like a dog! The hairs on the back of my neck stood up. I did not do the snarl, but I felt like it! This was a Bible college! Let me say that we are human beings at Bible college as well! So I was convicted and felt guilty about my attitude.

The sad thing was he always seemed to be on my table at meal times or next to me in the chapel. At every lecture I seemed to bump into him. I prayed, 'Please, Lord, show me how to get over this intense reaction because one day I shall explode'. I was afraid that I may resort to what I used to do at school where, although I knew it was wrong, I used to be quite aggressive. I wanted to be a boxer and a fighter. Here I was training for the ministry with those feelings welling up inside me. There was this guilt complex going on inside me because every time I saw him I wanted to give him my fist. So I went to one of the older Christians in the college to share my problem and offload. This is what I was told: 'Chris, there is only one answer. Pray that the Lord will bless him!' My spirit cried out in utter despair. 'Pray that the Lord will bless him?' Well, I am a willing guy and I gave it a go. I struggled with this, but I prayed for him and I prayed that God would bless him.

As I prayed I began to see him as a he really was. He was so insecure that he had to do all this boasting to boost his ego. I began to feel sorry for him and I realised I had won with the conflict I had. I learned to love him by praying for him.

Personality problems can cause all sorts of problems within and we have to hit them head on by praying for the person to be blessed, then the Lord can change us before he can change them. It takes time, but I have proved that it does work.

Let us have a look now at the enemy arrows that attack our relationships and what they do to us. When we feel the attack and it hurts, what we should do is take them to the cross of Jesus.

A very common arrow from the enemy is fear. Fear of not being liked or accepted. The Scripture tells us in 2 Timothy 1:7, 'God did not give us a spirit of timidity but a spirit of power, of love and of self-discipline'. So we know that this fear is an enemy attack and not from God. Jesus accepts us as we are and we need to accept each other in the same way.

We have already seen in Chris' testimony another arrow—that of wanting to prove oneself. And as we do this we affect others—we wound and hurt. We cause others to have conflict. The Scripture clearly states that salvation is not my works but grace through faith (Eph 2:8–9).

Another attack that affects our relationships is seeking to please people because we think by doing so we will not be hurt so much. Instead of pleasing God we start to please one another. It is a very serious problem in the church. We are not here to please one another, we are here to do the will of God. We need to understand where we are coming from and why we do what we do, otherwise we will get into a tangled mess and be worn out and exhausted.

Anger is another important factor and an arrow that can enter into relationships. Someone asks you to do something and you do it to please them, but inside you are angry because you did not want to do it! 'That is not what I wanted to do, but I couldn't say so, so I did it feeling really angry inside.' So you are in a big circle. If you continue to do that with all your relationships, then inside will build up a suppressed anger. This happens with a lot of people who come for counsel. Many have done this for years and have never been able to please themselves, let alone seek to please God.

Loneliness is the outcome of allowing arrows to penetrate the mind and so I cut myself off from people and friendships to protect myself.

Chris and I actually did this when we were hurt. We cut ourselves off from people and kept ourselves to ourselves. You do not want to ask for help any more and you become inward-looking. It causes wounds, fear and the sense of being an outcast. A wall of partition is built around you, which often manifests itself in body language, demeanour and speech. People who say things like, 'I am all right', or, 'There is nothing wrong with me!' can actually be very lonely inside. The wall is built so they will never be hurt again—hence isolation. This is very common in elderly people who have been hurt over the years. You can have twenty people sitting in a room yet all in their own little world of isolation, because over the years they have become more and more closed up until their mind starts to play tricks and reality slips away.

Christians, be encouraged; set your minds on things above and God will keep you from the world of isolation. I have seen Christians of ninety-six years old still mapping out their day around God and building relationships, so it *is* possible if we keep close to him. I remember another lovely Christian in her eighties who had requested that each day she was given time to spend with God before she was got up, and it was written into her card index for the day: 'Please leave time for this lady to have a prayer time before getting up in the mornings' One night she said to the nurse, 'I want to say goodbye, because I am going in the night', and the Lord took her in the night to be with him. She was ready to go.

The enemy fires arrows into the state of loneliness and exploits the weakness. A common way that you find people trying to cope with their loneliness is to have an animal as a pet. It depends on you. It does not answer back in a hurtful way and yet shows affection in response to your affection. I am sure you have found this to be true. Some elderly folk in the world have only one way to relate and that is through a pet, and when the pet dies often they too will give up. They depend on that animal to show the affection they have missed in life.

That is what we as Christians should be doing for one another—showing affection as a response to affection. Then we will be a true witness.

6

Help in Specific Relationships

Let us look at some of the difficult areas of relationships.
What about relating to non-Christians? We must first
realise that again our relationship with God comes first
and we seek to please God before any other human being.
We need to involve the Lord in the matter of who we
should relate to. I have often prayed and the Lord has sent
me to a specific person, and because the Lord was in it
from the beginning it has been all right.

The person who does not believe in Christ as Saviour has
only himself to please and the 'I want' syndrome is very
evident, especially in the caring profession. When I was
nursing, I saw this attitude of control very many times.
Often there is an attitude of 'don't give in' when someone
is taking up too much time or energy. We need to pray and
see what is behind a person's hard exterior. Often a hard or
difficult life has given way to bitterness and a desire to take
revenge on whoever is around at the time. There is nearly
always an unforgiving spirit and a hanging on to the hurt
and the pain. You then begin to feel sorry for that person.

I once had a problem with a nurse who was causing
others distress and was hence very disliked, and I had to
ask her what was wrong. She broke down in tears, telling
me the pain and the hurt that she was holding inside. I had
an opportunity to help her and that healing was to affect
those with whom she worked and cared for.

Even though a person has not yet accepted Jesus as
Saviour we can still help to heal them by using the

insights God has given us. We can be more understanding
and sympathetic to their needs rather than adding to their
hard exterior with the wrong attitude.

For many years, because of hurt within ourselves and
trying to please others, Christians have presented a judgemental gospel. If we look back to previous generations
there was often preached a judgemental gospel of 'You are
going to hell' without any feeling for the individual. It's
the church that needs to wake up to the fact that those
outside are going to hell and to seek to minister grace and
healing to the world outside rather than adding to the
already hurting spirit. What people need to know is that
there is a Saviour who loves and offers them security in
eternal life with him.

For many years the church protected itself from the
world, and I was brought up in a very safe place where
the world and the church hardly met. But if we are to reach
people, then we must not be afraid to rub shoulders with
all types of people and make friends and lasting relationships. We do not have to taste the sin, but we do need to
love the sinner. Jesus said, 'Be in the world but not of it.'
We need to get out there, go where the people are and
share Jesus at the level people are at, but we must not
lower our standards. We don't have to get drunk to please
people! We do not enter unwholesome relationships
because others are. The Scriptures warns us not to allow
our brother to stumble. That is our Christian brother, so we
need to protect the young Christian and the one with a
weakness. In our care groups or house groups we should
be able to share our weaknesses and be supported in a
loving environment. There are Christians who at present
are out there in the world and have lost their first love, due
to hurt and pain and hard words from their Christian
family (the church). We need to find them and bring
them home. If we show them the true love of Jesus and
meet them on their level, in time we will win. But we need
patience and prayer and support, if we are to accept each

other. We are not the judge, God is, and we need to remember that.

In our Christian walk we have come across many people, and I would like to share a testimony with you of a couple that we came across many years ago. They were a very ordinary couple: non-church-goers, hearts of gold, language a bit colourful, but we built up a friendship with this couple and they had no idea what my work was! Sometimes it is better not to advertise who and what you are, especially if you are ordained. In fact I often said jokingly that I was a caretaker. If they asked any further, I would tell them what I took care of! We went to have a cup of tea with this couple, who sat there enjoying their cigarettes, and we got talking. They knew we had some connection with the church and the husband started to share. If you take time to listen you can find out some very interesting things. He told us of a trip to Israel that he had made and how he had visited the Sea of Galilee where he had taken a boat out onto the water. This is what he said: 'I was actually on the same sea that ''he'' had been on. ''He'' was here and it gave me a strange and wonderful feeling. I sat where ''he'' sat!'

Here was a man who would not call himself a committed believer, but he had been touched by the Lord. Something happened to him in Israel and he said he really felt the presence of Jesus. That is the sort of opening that we can follow up by saying, 'Jesus is still around and wants you to know him'. This couple are still our friends and I pray one day they will find Jesus as Lord of their lives. You need to meet people where they are and approach them with their sense of humour. You don't have to use their language! If you have an open heart and a friendly nature, then you will win their affection and be able to share Jesus in a realistic way. We found eventually we could talk quite openly and even prayed with them when they had a need. I trust you will be encouraged to make relationships outside of the church;

relationships into which you can seek to bring a knowledge of the love and forgiveness of Jesus.

A word now about the Christian with an unbelieving partner. Some words of advice! Endeavour to meet them halfway; do not put them down in any way and certainly do not preach to them. We know of one man who took years to come through to Christ, but in the end he made a commitment. His wife was so keen, she was almost beside herself with anxiety and wrote out little texts and prayers, putting them under his pillow and by his breakfast, all to no avail. The sugar bowl had a text, the cereals had a text and so did his rolled up pyjamas! The more she tried the more he dug his heels in and became resistant. But when she was told to love her husband and submit to him, to spend time with him rather than be at the church every night of the week, and minister to his needs and take an interest in him, he began to change. The elders came and apologised for his wife being at the church too much and said they had suggested to her that she spent more time with him for she was still his wife and under his care as priest of the home. They also offered to come and talk to him about any difficulties that might arise and they encouraged the wife to love her husband.

Within weeks he was so impressed he responded to Christ. Praise God! So if you are into non-commanded works or trying to do God's work for him, then you are in danger of pushing your husband further away. Please do not bombard him with texts and prayers and do not let him find you in the bedroom praying out loud for him to be saved, saying what a wicked sinner he is! It will not help your situation.

The tragic truth is we are so desperate to see our partners won that we will try almost anything. That is understandable, but it will not help. God wants to save unconverted partners. Your prayers do not go unheard. However, because man has a free will and God has to allow us to come to our own realisation that we need him, it takes time. Let us let him do it. Let us find out what he wants us to do, and the Scripture tells us in 1 Peter that we will win our husbands over by the beauty of Jesus within and not by our words.

There is another important relationship within the body and that is the single person. We have found some of the most committed people in the church have been our single folk, but we must not take advantage of them. If you think you are being taken advantage of then you need to be free to say 'no'. Saying 'no' should not hurt us. In good relationships we should be able to say 'no' as well as 'yes' and then we are learning to please God rather than each other. We begin to appreciate that other people get tired and weary, so we need to be able to say 'no' to one another.

A Christian couple can be invaluable to a single person if they allow them into their lives and give them an open home to find friendship and fellowship. They need you to be able to enjoy the company of both sexes without feeling threatened and being misunderstood. We have always had a love for the single Christians and have had many share our home, whether for a day or for a few months. If you have a close and open relationship with your partner and trust each other, then you can open your home to the single Christian and give them a place of security and fellowship.

Older Christians need this ministry more than ever and the Scriptures encourage us to have an open home for our fellow Christians. Wherever we have been, our home has been open to any of our Christian friends. We do not put restrictions on them. Open relationships mean a sharing of hearts. We have actually had times of ourselves sleeping on the floor in the study to give someone a home for a while. We are talking here about committed Christians. To have unbelievers sharing your home is something for which you need wisdom and a clear direction from God. It is not recommended if you have a growing family.

I am going to include here some thoughts from a single Christian in one of our fellowships on relationships as she sees them. Janet has been working in Poland for a number of years and when she comes home to us she needs to know there is a family waiting for her in the church.

She says: 'It's very easy to look at everyone from our own perspective, but it's harder to put ourselves in others' shoes and try and realise the different needs and problems which others may have. We may need to recognise for example the constant commitments and tiredness of a couple with several young children, or the need of a single parent to sometimes enjoy an evening out with adult friends, free from the ties of the house and baby-sitting. Or think of the needs of an older person who can rarely get out of the house and enjoy fellowship with others.

'One thing which many singles enjoy is to be part of a family on occasions. I've often felt that I'd love to get to know families in the church more, but it can be difficult to know how. I've invited families for meals, but it's a rather nerve-racking experience because I am not used to cooking for more than one! And singles do not often have space for children to run around in. To be invited to join a family in their usual Sunday lunch or for coffee or for a chat in the evening is something many singles appreciate. So, remember; don't think that a single person won't want to come and see you! They would love it! They won't look for five-star cooking; they will come for company and fellowship.

'During these three years that I have lived in Poland, I've really appreciated the hospitality Chris and Jean have given me. Without it I could not have spent so much time in London during my holidays, keeping in touch with the church. It's been great to have a place where I know there will always be a welcome (and very often a packet of one of my favourite chocolate biscuits!), It's been good not to feel like a visitor but like part of the family—free to come and go but to join in with the washing-up and cooking.

'I suggest we all need to be open to giving hospitality to people in the church who are not part of our normal circle of friends. We need to look around and see singles, both young and old, couples and one-parent families and think about how we can show friendship—a cup of tea in the afternoon, a meal with a family, a small trip to our favourite eating house. Don't just look at people who are already your friends. Look at others and help to make the Christian family a living reality.'

There are other relationships that will be dealt with more fully in the next chapters, such as our relationships with teenagers and relationships in marriage.

7
Successful Marriage

After thirty years of marriage I can say that marriage is an institution I can heartily recommend! Having said that, in my teenage years I used to dream about being married and think: how wonderful, someone to look after me; someone to cook my meals and do my washing; someone to tidy up after me, perhaps even go out to work so that I won't have to work so hard myself. Ah! Bliss!

Marriage has fulfilled some of my expectations, but it has fulfilled far more than I really dreamed possible and I learned very early on that my quiet strong will and expectations were in direct conflict with someone else's extrovert, strong will and there had to be some give and take! Nevertheless, we are still here and want to recommend marriage to you! We want to share some of our experiences.

Christian marriage is a commitment made on earth and in heaven. I asked the Lord to show me my wife. Actually we met in a farmyard and it was easy to distinguish her from the cattle, the sheep and the pigs! She was the answer to my prayers. We were actually on a youth weekend run by the 'National Young Life Campaign' which in those days was reaching many young people with the gospel by holding weekends on a large farm near Oxford. We were divided into washing-up groups and there we were in the same group.

Jean should not really have been there at all that weekend. It was a miracle that she was able to come. She had been working on night duty as a student nurse and although she had requested the weekend off she had been refused. So on the Friday she was feeling very disappointed when another nurse asked her if she would change duties with her because she needed the time off on the following Monday. So Jean at the very last minute, having been up all night on duty, rushed to Oxford. I had been praying and asking the Lord that my wife would be a nurse and I had the strong impression her name would be Jean, and she would have dark hair and brown eyes. I even asked the Lord to confirm she was the right one by her going on the same holiday as me at a Baptist Youth summer school in Worthing!

The first afternoon, after we had managed to get away from everyone else, I found out that all these things fitted into place, even to the same holiday, although the dates only overlapped for a few days. So after sharing our lives for four hours I knew she was the right one for me, but we would have to wait a few years before getting married! I knew that this was the one for me, and the next morning we were up very early praying together. Now that is a very romantic story and although true it is not the usual way things happen.

Apart from our Christian experience, there are two ingredients for marriage that I want to underline here. When you get married it is a legal agreement—the law is involved—and there should also be love. Very often when the relationship is strained to the limit you may not feel you love your partner—that's when the rolling-pin comes out! Law comes into operation; you are not permitted to do what you want or to walk out or leave. As Christians you are also in a covenant relationship with God, and you covenanted together before God and before your friends that you would be man and wife. You made a testimony and a stand as you said your vows; and I believe if you give your word you should want to keep it, even if it costs you. There are some circumstances where it is impossible to keep your word, but you should in most cases do your utmost to keep it.

Trust and love are all-important in this covenant relationship. If you cannot trust someone, how can you love them? If there is no trust, any relationship will crumble. If you do not trust you will not share things or want to communicate. There is always the element of doubt as to how far you dare to go. To what lengths do you have to go to trust someone? Trust is what all marriages need to build. Love is not just physical attraction; love means a trust being built in as well. I thought my wife was the best girl I had seen that weekend, but without a trust being built up as well, our love would not last. I still believe my wife to be the best because I still love her! I tell husbands that if you do not think your wife is the most beautiful person then there is something wrong with them (the husbands that is!). Some say, 'But I must be real'. Yes, and romantic as well!

It takes work and effort to keep a relationship alive. So love and trust are all-important and you need an open relationship. I counsel many folk and I have found that many times the relationship breaks down due to lack of communication.

This story was shared with me about a man whose wife told him that if he did not go and see their family doctor who was a committed Christian she would leave him that day. So he went to the doctor's, although he could not understand why he needed to go. He went off quite dismayed. He could not think of anything he had done to upset her. That evening he visited the doctor, who said to him, 'Now sit down and tell me about your wife and about yourself'. So he proceeded to say that everything was fine, that there were no problems that he could see and he had no idea what was wrong. The doctor then asked him to share a typical day with him. So he shared, 'At 7.30 am, after getting out of bed, I go to the bathroom for a wash and shave. I then come downstairs where my breakfast is ready on the table and I eat it reading the news-paper. Then I have a quick listen to the news and the weather before I go off to work, giving my wife a quick kiss as I go out of the door. My wife gives me my sandwiches that she has made and I go off to catch the bus for work. I work all morning and eat my sandwiches during my lunch hour. I start writing up my records, then work all afternoon, bringing some more work home with me in the evening. As soon as I arrive home my meal is on the table and I eat it listening to the news. As soon as I have finished I go upstairs to do some more work for three hours. When I have finished my wife brings me a hot drink and I give her another kiss and we go to bed. That is my day, Monday to Friday. Weekends I play golf.'

The doctor said to him, 'If you do not learn to listen to your wife and talk to her, your marriage will be finished. If you do not spend time together enjoying each other's company then there is no hope.'

The man answered, 'But she knows I love her. She doesn't want for anything. I give her money and I am faithful to her. What is the point in talking? She knows I love her!'

This man had a lesson to learn: that communication is part of relationship; in fact a major part. It's so important to talk and to share if you want a successful marriage.

'Husbands love your wives as you do yourself.' Listen to her, relate to her. I have learned that my wife gets things from God that I miss. There is no competition in marriage. We share together. In Genesis God provides a help-meet for Adam—a partner who is an equal and a partner to walk with hand in hand (that is what the Hebrew word 'help-meet' meant). What the woman lacks, the man will make up and vice versa.

Our relationship with God undergirds every relationship we have, whether it be husbands and wives or any other relationship. If we are united with our heavenly Father then our relationship with our partner will be that much more fruitful and blessed. As Chris' wife I can remember days when, as I shared in a previous chapter, I did not want to walk with God because I was so hurt, and during that time Christ suffered as well. Our relationship was strained and often communication broke down. We still loved one another, but we were more distant because my relationship with God was not right (see Gen 2:18–24; Mt 19:5–6; Mk 10:6–9). If we are agreed together, then we can move mountains. In your home you have great power if you both agree. That makes life exciting because as you are united in prayer you can lay problems before the Lord that alone would be difficult. We need to say here that any two people who agree can pray and have the same effect if their hearts are one; so if you are single and reading this, then join with a friend and start praying together for your problems to be resolved. We are made in the image of God (Gen 1:26–28). If we are made in his image then we need to be like him. To be like him, we need to know him and the only way to know our heavenly Father is to talk to him and read his word.

Loving one another is so important in marriage. When you first tie the knot, love is high on the list, and before you get married it explains and solves everything! You are so dreamy and so in love you could never fall out, but a week after the honeymoon things start to change, as your wills begin to surface. Then self begins to emerge as you are determined that he says 'sorry' first or vice versa! I remember packing a suitcase and walking around the block while Chris followed closely by in the mini van we had, to make sure I was all right. We have often laughed since about that incident. We have no idea what it was all about! I wasn't really leaving him. I was trying to see how far I could go! I don't know what we achieved, but I suppose at the time we tried to prove something to each other. After walking around the block we both crept back in, frightened that the landlady might see us and wonder what was wrong! Asking Chris since what it was all about, he says that it was because he was right! That is exactly what happens when two people become one: they both want to be right. Over the years you learn to listen to each other and seek to discover what is the right way by giving your thoughts and ideas to the Lord in prayer. Sometimes it means giving in and admitting fault. Other times it means admitting that although right, our attitude was not one of love.

As a loving husband I have found that more important than the love letters I leave under the pillow, or the bunch of flowers that I have never bought but picked from someone else's garden (with their permission, of course) is to tell her face to face that you love your wife and that she is beautiful. The Scripture tells us that pleasant words are a healing to our flesh, so say good things to your partner. The world is full of negative words of bitterness and hate. Let us show by our relationships that we truly love one another and trust each other. I believe that if we love and encourage one another it builds security and a lasting relationship. It also builds confidence because you begin to realise that someone believes in you and accepts you.

Husbands should not only be telling wives that they are loved, wives need to tell their husbands that they love them and that they are the best man in the world! There is such a thing as poetic licence! The Bible encourages us to love our neighbour as ourselves, not to have a proud selfish love for ourselves but a healthy love of ourselves which will then spill into our marriage, as we are one flesh.

We need to love our partner as ourselves, protecting them as if they were part of us. Together we are one. We may not always agree, but we are still one and need to communicate to each other. 'Speak to me!' and 'Listen to me!' are words that ring true!.

Several months ago we were flying to Ireland to help in counselling, and on our return journey we were sitting in the lounge in Belfast International Airport awaiting our flight home. There on the television screen was an episode of *Coronation Street*. Jack was shouting at his wife Vera and it came over loud and clear in the airport lounge. 'If I've told you once I've told you a thousand times . . . you never listen to me.' I thought, 'Ah! I have heard that before many times over in counselling sessions–'You never listen to me', or, 'She does not listen to me'.

Communication means one is talking and the other listening and then roles change and the other talks while their partner listens. Listening is not keeping your mind on the television set or the newspaper. It means undivided attention. When you get that far away look in your eyes you cannot hide it from your wife! Talking and listening are essential for an open and honest relationship. Honesty is also very important. It is not a licence to say what you like in a hurtful or insensitive way, but I do believe we can be honest in a loving way. When you feel loved and accepted by the other person you can accept their loving criticism because you know they genuinely want your best. It does not cause a wound or an arrow to penetrate the heart, but if you speak without love then you will wound and hurt and this is true in any relationship, whether it be marriage or a Christian friendship.

One way to keep your marriage alive is to do things together. Washing-up together can be fun as you chat and share. Gardening can be fun together! I remember our first attempts at house decoration were great fun and we laughed at our mistakes–which were quite a few!

I can get on well with open people because I know where I am with them, but if you have a partner who is closed up, then you have no idea what they are thinking or feeling and it will take time and patience to win their confidence again and you may even need a third person to counsel and guide you both. It is so difficult to know if they love you if they never show feelings.

This British culture has a lot to answer for when we talk
about having to 'keep a stiff upper lip', controlling our
feelings. It is wrong and causes damage to ourselves as
well as those we love. I am not saying we should go
around in public always displaying our feelings!
Obviously there is a time and place, but the little whisper
in my wife's ear when no one is looking will make her feel
wanted and accepted.

Encouraging one another is scriptural. Share your
thoughts and feelings with each other. If you cannot share
with the one you love then how can you communicate to
this world in which we live? If you feel over-responsible
for your partner or over-protective, then you will put a
stranglehold upon them. They need space to be themselves. You are one, but you are also individuals with
needs and requirements in life that may be different.
You will need to sit down together and talk through
your needs and desires together and listen to each other.

Do not seek to control or manipulate your partner. This
is done in so many relationships. We have met people who
have learned to turn on the tears to get their own way,
knowing it will make their husband give in. That's control
and manipulation. We have seen situations where the
husband is right at all costs and after a blazing row one
went to the wardrobe and took out the trousers and said,
'The one who wears these is boss'. Unfortunately they
were his wife's trousers! So when he said, 'Do you agree
that the one who wears these is boss?' she said 'yes!'

There are husbands who lay down the law continually,
especially in Christian homes where they say, 'I am the
head of the home, so you do as you are told and submit'.
There are times when as head of the home the husband has
to make difficult decisions and it should be so. But on the
whole there should be a mutual submission and a love that
comes from the Lord, who himself is head over us.

There are men who control their wives and their wives
become slaves, and there are some husbands who become

slaves. We have counselled some, even in Christian homes, who have resorted to physical violence to get their own way. What we see here is a direct attack of the enemy, using a very strong spirit of control and manipulation. The person needs to repent and be set free. With mutual trust and co-operation there is light, but there will be a need for counsel and help from a confidential source.

How many reading this said the wedding vows 'in sickness and in health? I have learned during the years what that means. Recently, when Jean was being examined by a doctor for abdominal pain, he asked the usual questions to which Jean replied, 'No, that has gone . . . No, that has been taken too'. When he had finished he said to her, 'Well, there isn't much left that could be wrong. All the spare parts have already gone!'

I know, because every time she came out of hospital after yet another operation I had to look after her. Our first year in one pastorate was spent with Jean having surgery and the people in the village began to think the place did not suit her, especially when after returning home from having a plaster off her leg for a ruptured Achilles she landed up with chronic pain in her gall bladder which was promptly removed! There I was cooking and cleaning and coping with four children and sleeping by her side to help her. I learned what 'in sickness and in health' really meant. I realised that work around the house is difficult to do and quite demanding and exhausting, let alone looking after someone sick in bed as well.

Life together is not all fun and play. There are difficult times and we need to realise that when we enter into a partnership for life. There are times when we change roles and help because the situation demands it. Sometimes we have to grit our teeth and just go through the difficult times, knowing that the Lord will bring us through, despite the fact that we are so tired we want to sit down and be served, not crawl to the sink!

Remember the lady who put texts everywhere to get her husband saved? I want to recommend that you leave love notes for your wife or husband to read under pillows or on the table for when they come home. Remember to tell her first that you love her! I went out to Guyana last year and in my suitcase was a note ready for me to read when I unpacked all those thousands of miles away from my wife. Appreciate each other, particularly you men; learn to appreciate your wives and show them you love them. You never know what might happen. You may find you have a wife who is far more sweet and amiable than you thought possible!

Before we finish this chapter on marriage we need to look at some of the problems that occur, such as when our partner is not a Christian. Much of what we have shared does still apply; communication, appreciation and learning to love, but there are obviously more difficulties that arise. One thing we have emphasised is that you will not win him over by putting texts in sugar bowls and under his pillow! The Scripture in 1 Peter says that we should love our husband and win him over with a quiet and submissive spirit. In other words, we do not try to manipulate or control the situation but just love him and seek to find ways of serving him that will show our faith and love. We mention it this way around because it usually is a non-Christian husband, although we have met some cases of non-Christian wives, and the same applies. You will not win anyone by arguing, but by showing a pattern of life which communicates love and understanding. This does not mean spending every night at the church but rather being willing to go out with him as well, even though it cuts across the most exciting meeting of the week. Trying to drag him along will only put his back up. But that does not mean you cannot ask him if he will come with you. Spend time with your husband and he is more likely to spend time coming to something you enjoy. If you became a Christian after you were married, then I am sure the Lord will complete the work he has started in your home, so be encouraged to continue to pray and seek God's help in the relationship.

If we deliberately went into a marriage with a non-Christian, then we have gone against what God intended, for he warns us not to be unequally yoked. Many come to us when they realise their mistake and we counsel them to repent and ask God to forgive. This is sometimes enough to bring their partner through, but for others there is the pain of divorce or separation as their partner leaves. If a Christian has deliberately ignored the Scriptures, it has created great difficulties, but be encouraged that God forgives.

I had one person come to me and ask me to marry a Christian to a non-Christian and I refused as I feel I cannot encourage what I believe in Scripture to be against what God wants for the believer. I will marry two non-Christians or two Christians, but not a non-Christian to a Christian. I will bless them and pray for them, but not marry them.

Even in my own family I have had to refuse, which is very hard. It sounds a hard line to take, but I have learned through experience that if I break God's law that he lays down for our good, then I am encouraging perhaps another break-up or another difficult marriage, and I am also being disobedient to God myself, which could have an effect on my relationship with him. I want to do things God's way. There are some scriptures which back up what I am saying (for example, Eph 5:21–33 and 1 Pet 3:1–9). If you read these passages you will also find further recommendations.

Another problem in marriage is one that comes up in counselling: 'We cannot agree on anything'. Then that is where you have to start by agreeing to differ! Do not let the sun go down on any dispute. If you cannot agree, then accept each other's point of view and admit that probably you are both right or wrong! There are very few times in our thirty years of married life when we have tried to go to sleep without speaking to each other. In fact it lasted about twenty minutes at the most before we said 'sorry' and let go. The hardest part is that both think the other should say 'sorry' first. Well, one of you has to give in, or try saying it together!

Bad communication is better than none at all. We hear people who say, 'We never have a cross word or a difference of opinion'. It makes you wonder what their relationship is really like. We need to talk to each other, and at some point we will disagree, but it's far better to sort it out than not talk at all. It would be better not to argue, but communication is so important that it's better to argue than keep silent. Then the true problem sometimes emerges as you realise that you did not think your wife or your husband felt like that.

The main time that we ever had arguments when the children were small was on holiday, travelling in the car. Jean will tell you how she was always convinced we were going the wrong way and that she was right and I was equally convinced my directions were correct! Does this ring a bell? Jean was trying to map-read and I did not believe her and then realised afterwards that she could read the map after all! We have to learn to accept that our partner can be right as well as ourselves.

Over-responsibility, over-protectiveness and control in marriage can become problems which will need dealing with when recognised, as these will develop into those enemy arrows or enemy spirits that will steal and destroy your relationship. When you begin to see that you are giving the enemy freedom to break up your relationship, you will be more on your guard to protect what God has given you. As you recognise the attack, begin to deal with it. Over-responsibility or being over-protective are enemy arrows, so deal with them.

If you have ever counselled non-Christians in a marriage guidance set-up you will know what we are saying is true, as you will have heard the control and strong will coming over. You can actually learn to pick up the patterns of manipulation and control and strong over-protectiveness and you can see the enemy playing havoc with a couple. Marriage is ordained by God and Satan is into breaking up marriages. Whether they are Christian or not he just wants to see anything God has ordained broken up. If we see this we will be more on our guard to protect what God has given.

If as you read this you realise that these things are present in your own situation, then you will need prayer and help in dealing with them, but a lot can be achieved just by recognising the pattern that has developed and confessing the sin to God, renouncing and repenting. This will release the situation.

Another problem we often come across is when one partner has lost their first love in the Lord and therefore the other feels spiritually alone. Even if your partner is not committed, don't forsake your own prayer time. Don't allow their lack of trust in God to affect your relationship with God, for it is so important that you stay firm, other-wise again Satan will think he is winning a victory and will not let go. Don't nag your partner to change; just pray for them and allow God to work. Give your feelings and hurt over to God and he will in his time answer your prayers, because if you keep that quietness in your spirit and love them and serve them in Jesus then you will give opportunity for the Holy Spirit to work in their lives. So often we stand in the way and block the spiritual channel with our own way, thinking we know best. Ask God to change you as well!

Personality and character clashes can be overcome if the hearts of both of you are set on God and you love each other; then he will change you. When we first met we were told by friends that your relationship would not last, for we were so different and opposites in a way that was not healthy. I was more outgoing and extrovert and Chris was the quiet one. If it had been the other way round no one would have said anything, but because I was the organiser and the communicator everyone said we were in for trouble!

It took a lot for me to change over the years and realise where arrows were getting into our relationship. It also took a lot for Chris to realise the need to come forward as the husband and priest in his home and not to feel threatened by me or leave things to me.

Over the years he has set me free to be myself. He has not put me down. I am able to speak and share and he knows and trusts me that I am not taking over his role for I respect him and his position.

The more you learn to trust one another and the more you recognise your own character and understand yourself, the easier it becomes to relate to each other in the correct way. The Lord can use you and set you free.

Christian wives, you don't have to be under the thumb of a dominating husband; husbands, you don't have to hide behind a dominating wife. God can change you to be what he intended you to be. When you trust and set each other free, you will find such blessing in your marriage and achieve so much more for God.

The power and influence that lies in the hand of a wife is tremendous for good or for evil. She has the ability to open a trap door through which her husband can fall to despair, or to erect a ladder by which he can climb to achievement and success. Blessed is the man with a good and godly wife who understands the influence that lies within her grasp and co-operates with the Almighty in making her husband the man of God.

Two examples from Scriptures of godly wives are Sarah and Ruth. Both are commended in the Scriptures and both are linked to the family line of David and Jesus Christ, Sarah being the wife of Abraham and Ruth the wife of Boaz. If you compare their lives with Jezebel, who married King Ahab in the book of Kings, you will know that

Jezebel led her husband, did everything for him, controlled him, wrote letters, lied for him, murdered on his behalf and manipulated people. She was so bad and wicked that she led a fine warrior king to be as evil as she was herself and God cursed the family. The whole family was destroyed because King Ahab abdicated his role as a husband and as a leader of the people of Israel because he allowed his wife to dominate, manipulate and control him.

By the reverse, if you have a wife who is behind you and prays for you and encourages you, then, because God blesses unity and co-operation, you can realise your full potential. A good Christian marriage is a picture of the relationship between God and his church, and the bottom line of family life is the relationship of man and wife. Wives have been very much under-rated in many Christian circles, but read the Bible and find the commendation that God gives to godly wives, especially Proverbs 31. 'He who finds a godly wife finds a treasure.' I know what I do when I get my hands on a treasure. I hang on to it!

We trust that in this chapter we have encouraged you to keep your relationships with each other alive and that you will have some understanding of your own problems as well as other people's. God wants marriage. He ordained it. He is right behind you and therefore will help you. You are walking with him, so hang in there and see what God can do.

8

My Own Worst Enemy: Myself

As you will see from the chapter title we have made a very plain statement: 'Our worst enemy is ourselves!' We must accept responsibility for our speech and actions, although we are shaped by the past. So whenever people say, 'I cannot help it. That's the way I was brought up, I have had a bad deal and wrong events in my life, hence this is why I behave like I do', that is no excuse. It may help us understand why we do certain things, but in the end we have to face the fact that we can grieve God by the way we behave. So we need to accept the responsibility for what we say and what we do.

Let us look at a few passages of Scripture that will set the scene. We need to understand from the very beginning that we always need to turn to the Jesus of the cross.

> Surely he has borne our griefs and carried our sorrows; yet we esteemed him stricken, smitten by God, and afflicted. But he was wounded for our transgressions, he was bruised for our iniquities; upon him was the chastisement that made us whole, and with his stripes we are healed. All we like sheep have gone astray; we have turned every one to his own way; and the Lord has laid on him the iniquity of us all (Is 53:4–6, RSV).

Psalm 51:6 says: 'Surely you desire truth in the inner parts; you teach me wisdom in the inmost place.' If you have the truth of God empowered by the Spirit of God within your heart, you will know that the truth will set you free. Although I have only quoted one verse, the whole of the psalm is beneficial for you to read.

Psalm 91 offers some words of encouragement: 'Because he cleaves to me in love, I will deliver him' (v. 14, RSV). That is wonderful news–I can be delivered. 'I will protect him, because he knows my name' (v. 14, RSV). That reminds us of the armour of God. 'When he calls to me, I will answer him' (v. 15, RSV). That's a reminder of the importance of prayer. 'I will be with him in trouble, I will rescue him and honour him. With long life I will satisfy him, and show him salvation' (vv. 15–16, RSV). Jesus Christ came to bring us life in all its abundance and in all its fullness.

Let us now look at how we are made up. All of us will identify with voices from the past. In the innermost part of our minds we have stored all the voices from our child-hood. We could imagine this to be like the attic in our house, where we keep all old photos and letters. If our parents were not putting positive input into our lives as children but were sowing hatred, discord, perhaps abuse or violence, anger or negative words, or perhaps they were just not there when we needed them, this means that as a child, to some degree or other, we were deprived and the attitudes and statements our parents made impressed upon us and we still remember them. They have lodged in our mind and at times we bring them to the surface like looking over old boxes in the attic. What we need to do is clear out the rubbish, the things that should not be retained, and keep only the best. When we are moving house that is what we do, isn't it? Our minds need to be wiped clean from the bad events of the past so that we can live free and healthy lives in the present.

Most of the time we can live normal happy lives until we are reminded of the past or the repression we feel affects us. The experiences we had in our childhood and over the past years of our life affect the way we respond to everyday living today. Hence if we do not feel we are getting the best out of our lives as Christians it may be that we need to start clearing out some old dusty room that Jesus has never been allowed in and therefore has not swept clean. Remember we are not talking about our soul, which is saved, but we are talking about our minds and emotions that go to make up our being and have a profound effect on the way we behave.

On the other hand, if our parents on the whole loved us, supported us and encouraged us then our present life will be good, and accepting ourselves will be much easier. We will be able to step out in confidence. It means that our attic is full of good memories that far outweigh the poor ones. It's very true that what we receive as children affects what we are as adults.

You may have heard the story of the family who through the generations were told you never put your coat on the bed or your hat on the table, and that had been instilled in the minds of the children throughout their lives.

The third generation decided to ask why. They asked their parents and they did not know, so they asked their grandparents and the answer was quite simple. In years gone by hygiene was much more difficult and if you put your hat on the table, lice from the hat might get onto the table where you ate, so you did not put your hat on the table! If you put your coat on the bed a similar thing might happen and lice may get into the bedclothes!

There was a very logical explanation, but this voice was so strong it had been passed down from generation to generation and had been obeyed even though it did not have the same reasoning any more!

This is just an amusing example of what can be handed down, but there are far worse things that affect us deeply. I have counselled many who have heard from childhood, 'You will never be any good. You are hopeless,' and so they never have been any good and have given up. The child thought they were worthless and a failure and so the adult thinks the same.

We must not blame our parents completely for these attitudes because often it is something like the hat and coat, that has been said for many years, by grandparents and back even further than that. Sometimes we can find the reason. Perhaps a past relative turned out to be bad and caused the family heartache and from then on any children were labelled the same. They were also thought to be no good, hence the voice starts to be heard down through generations until one day one person becomes a Christian and realises that he can achieve something, so repents of listening to this wrong attitude and is cut free from the bondage that has held him all his life. We have seen this happen time and again when a person has forgiven their parents and renounced the words and asked the Holy Spirit to set them free.

The behaviour of our parents, grandparents, friends and other relatives does affect us, especially if they all say similar negative things to us. We need prayer and setting free from the past.

Some of the things we have written about in previous chapters do overlap with what we are writing here, but as you read again you will begin to form a picture of yourself, and where you need help.

We have explained to you the effect on us of losing our first child at the age of one year and for many years after we heard voices saying, 'Why did you not do more?' Voices like these can haunt, and if they are not dealt with they can cause us to overact with any future baby and become over-protective.

This happened to us and we had to recognise what we were doing and give the situation into the hands of the Lord. Past experiences have a strong influence on the present, so we had to pray through the experience and forgive ourselves for thinking we might have done more, and cut ourselves off from the 'what if' syndrome, giving our son back to the Lord and accepting that he was in control.

A more up-to-date testimony happened while we were sharing this series. In the middle of the series we were to have a break and during that break everything seemed to go wrong! Jean's mother died during the week and Jean herself was taken ill. The idea was that we have a rest, but this was not to be. At first we thought this was an enemy attack, but then we thought, 'No, God is in control of everything and this is the right time for Mum to be called home'. We can so easily lock ourselves into situations where we go into a spiral of thought: 'This is an enemy attack . . . Why me, Lord? . . . How can I cope? I will not get into this mess again . . .' And so it goes on, getting more and more negative. What we have to do is stop it before it gets to the stage where we cannot let go. We have allowed the enemy arrows to invade the thought-life and are giving in because of the emotional crisis. God is able to give the strength. He has promised that he can strengthen us in all situations and so I can testify that he strengthened us to continue the series.

Let Jean continue the story . . . On the night my mother was taken ill we were actually visiting Chris' father, who was recovering from an operation in a nursing home. The other voices that started to attack me were the doctors and nurses who, when we did ring about my mother, did not give any indication that she was seriously ill. We were told there was no urgency and we arranged to travel the next day, only to find that it was too late. The voice that springs to mind says, 'Why? Why did I not go? Why was I not told?' So all these voices crowded my mind, not of the past but of the present, and they too needed to be dealt with, otherwise they would start to affect the way I would live in the future, causing panic and anxiety.

Here I was in the middle of what I had been teaching for the past weeks on how to cope and how to deal with the enemy when attacked. It is not the event that is the enemy attack, but it's the way we allow the enemy to use the event.

I needed my helmet firmly on! The Lord then showed me that my mother had always feared death and if I had been there she would have known she was dying, but as it happened she slipped away peacefully and he showed me that he was there with my mother. For her sake I had to say, 'Thank you, Lord, you were with her even though I was not', and I had to reverse what was being said to me.

In the same way we have to face the fact that life is life—an event is not necessarily enemy attack. Death does happen, and we as Christians are not different from anyone else in this respect. We have to live in this world and accept what comes to us, but with one big bonus: we have a Saviour and Lord who has trod this path and will help us through and strengthen us if we allow him to.

We have to face suffering and sorrow and cannot always look for someone to blame. We have a responsibility ourselves to lean on Jesus and look to him for strength and support, putting on the armour that he has provided us with. When we start listening to other voices, whether they be from the past or from the present, let us first of all examine ourselves and put on our armour so that we can dismiss what is not helpful to us. It is not easy. When I eventually found out that my mother had had cancer for weeks and no one knew, I cried, and I felt so hurt that she had suffered pain, but again, after the grief, I had to let go and thank the Lord that my mother was in his safe-keeping.

We are not writing what we have picked up from others, we are writing what we ourselves have experienced, and we are in this together. This is reality and Jesus is able to bring us through if we will listen to this voice. The still small voice or the loud thunder, whatever it may be, God will speak and encourage us to go on with him. We will only hear his voice when we start to reject all the other voices that we hear.

If you find you have one voice that keeps coming back like a stuck record that you cannot get rid of, then please seek help to be set free. Write it down and share it with us if you have no one else, whether it be abuse or through tragedy or a bad event in your life. It can stop you from sleeping or from making rational decisions and needs the healing touch of Jesus.

Let us look now at a lighter side of ourselves: 'Do I like myself?' Do I know who I am?'

God has made us in his image. Whether we are black or white we are made in the image of God. We have known black people who wish they were white because they feel they would be treated better, and we have known white people who cannot stand themselves at all! Please accept yourself as you are. God made you and he wants you to be proud of your colour and race.

Genesis 1:26 says this: 'Then God said, "Let us make man in our image . . . and let them rule over the fish of the sea and the birds of the air . . ." so God created man in his own image . . . male and female he created them'.

When God created us we were perfect human beings. God accepts us just as we are. It is a sin not to accept ourselves, for God accepts us exactly as we are, whether our nose is big or small or whether we are fat or thin, big or small. Our looks are not important to God. It is what we are inside that counts and whether our hearts are in harmony with him.

We have met people who will not look in the mirror because they feel they are not worth looking at, and yet God loves and accepts them. It is vital that you accept yourself, otherwise you are making out that you know better than God! We as Christians really need to learn to accept ourselves, for the danger is that we will treat others the same as ourselves and not accept them either. We will start to see the faults in other people and compare them with ourselves, so it's very important that we take hold of what God is saying here because it affects the whole of our lives.

It does not mean that God will not change us, or want us to change, for as we become more like him we may well want to be different. We may well be a healthier person if we lost some weight, and God can help us to do that if we bring it to him in prayer, but that should not be the priority way of life for us as Christians. As we grow closer to the Lord, then discipline in life becomes an easier task and we can change a great deal just by being closer to Jesus and listening to his commands. Our main aim is to be like Jesus and if we make that our priority then the love of Jesus will shine out of our lives and what we look like will take second place.

Many of you will have read the books of Joni Eareckson who had an accident as a teenager and was paralysed from the neck down, yet her personality and faith far outshine her disabilities. Her inner radiance comes from her love for Jesus which has compensated for all her shortcomings. Her life could have been wasted and she could have been forgotten, but because of her faith and trust in the Lord her life has been a tremendous testimony to many. Her face radiates the beauty and love of the Lord so much that her body is not noticed. She is a beautiful person. Joni has learned the secrt of accepting herself as she is. She is at peace with God and is not listening to the voices of the past that could have destroyed her present life. She is not listening to the voice of 'Why me?' or 'Why have I not been healed?' What she is doing is resting in Jesus.

Let us now look at some of the experiences that can happen to us in life and how we react to them.

What happens when you are told you will not have a job by the end of the month? This is a very relevant situation today and it is good that we examine our reactions. First, there is the initial shock to the system that we feel, whatever the bad news that is given to us. This is a natural response, but it is also one where we will have a weakness for enemy arrows to attack. So what do we do? Do we say, 'I must be a worthless person if my boss does not want me', or 'Why me?' or, 'Why not someone else?' or, 'I must be useless?' Does our mind start to dwell on why we have been singled out. Do we then progress into, 'I will never find another job. If my present boss does not want me, then no one else will either', or, 'Everything happens to me'?

If we continue to think like this then the consequence will be, 'The world is a terrible place, everyone is out of work and unhappy'. Depression sets in or we become a very angry and bitter person. If the depression does not go or the anger gets worse, we start to dwell on all things that have happened to us. The world is full of injustice and we are going to get what we want, and selfishness sets in. We become a very negative person and very sad, losing friends who cannot cope with us and losing our self-worth, not accepting ourselves as we are.

So how can we change the spiral? First, by recognising what is happening. The enemy is playing on our weakness and shock at losing our job and will continue to do so unless we bring the whole problem to the foot of the cross and thank the Lord for the job we had and ask him to forgive us for our anger and hurt and to help us to see the next step. It may be that God can use us in the church to help the pastor. If you live in the city, I can assure you there is a great deal you can do. It may be that God will guide you to another open door for work, but whatever, he is still in control of your life and can provide for you. In Christ we can cope. It's not the bad event that affects us, but all the ways in which we interpret it from then on. As Christians we are going to be tempted to have negative thoughts, but we must remind ourselves of the helmet of salvation which is there to protect us and keep us in peace as our mind is stayed on him. If we do not allow God to heal our innermost thoughts then they will eat us away.

We have met folk in their seventies and eighties who have hung on to bitterness and anger for years and years, and now they are bitter, miserable people who are not loved or accepted. They have been eaten away and now believe they are worthless. Joni could have been like that, but she chose to hand her pain to the one who is able to heal and to set free. Inside she is spiritually free and therefore can sing with power and real anointing from God.

Let us look more fully into the sin of rejecting ourselves. If we continue to do this we are actually sinning against God: 'Accept one another, then, just as Christ accepted you, in order to bring praise to God' (Rom 15:7). 'Yet to all who received him, to those who believed in his name, he gave the right to become children of God–children . . . born of God' (Jn 1:12).

You are children born of God so what right have you got to reject yourself if God has accepted you through his Son Jesus Christ? We need to love ourselves and love one another. The Scripture tells us to do this. We need to love and accept each other as Christ loves us.

Years ago, when my parents were courting, they came across an old Eastender called 'Lofty'–a man of the road. He lived in the city of London on the streets.

Lofty was a tramp who wore rags as clothes. One day, he found himself in the church at Spitalfields, where he accepted Jesus into his life to be his Lord and Saviour. Lofty was welcomed and accepted by the Christians in the church. They showed him love and kindness. My father was one of those who made friends with Lofty. No one told Lofty that he should wash or get some new clothes–they accepted him as he was–but slowly a transformation came over him as Jesus changed him from the inside. We can do damage by trying to change people without waiting for Jesus to change them first. I remember my parents telling me how Lofty came up to my father and said, 'Guv, could you spare a clean collar for me?' and my father gave him a lovely white collar that he wore on his dirty ragged shirt! He was so proud of his new collar and then he asked for a tie and so it went on until he was dressed in respectable clothes for Jesus.

He had no money, there was no social security in those days and he lived on what he was given by others, but when my parents were married he gave them a present. It was a china dog which we called Bonzo. I still have it in my possession as it is precious, even though it has been broken and mended. The dog represented all that Lofty had in the world. It cost sixpence from Woolworths, and that is the old sixpence which is just two-and-a-half pence today, and it was a way of saying 'thank you' for all the help they had given him. The Lord Jesus can change you if you let him.

Only as we accept ourselves as we really are can God change us into what he wants us to be. It's not the outward appearance of wearing a wig or dyed hair, but looking to see if there is an inward reason for doing. It is the inward feelings and reactions that often need the forgiveness and repentance or healing. We need to examine our lives and see if there is not a degree of non-acceptance. It may be the area of intellect—we are not as clever as we think we should be. We think we are thick or stupid. Jesus welcomes us as we are when we accept him into our lives, so who are we that we cannot do the same?

Another area which causes problems in our Christian life is blaming Satan when actually it's our own self which is at fault. The Bible is very clear that for the dozens and dozens of times where God in his power and his majesty, in his freedom, deliverance and salvation is mentioned, there is very little reference to Satan and his power. I believe this is significant. I believe that gives us a good guide on how much we should talk about Satan that is, not a lot! When we talk about him, he receives that as worship of him. You notice that Jesus gave him a very short shrift. When challenged Jesus said, 'It is written: thou shalt not . . .' and gave a word of Scripture.

Sometimes people have a lot of bother because they give a lot of credibility to Satan. I know he is a thief and a robber and out to destroy, but that comes from

exactly the same passage where Jesus said, 'I came that
they might have life, and have it abundantly' (Jn 10:10,
RSV). This chapter concentrates more on the abundance of
life than on what the enemy will do.

If you read through some of the occasions when the
enemy is mentioned they are so few compared with how
many times Jesus is mentioned. Let's make a lot about
Jesus and his conquering victorious power and be rather
silent when it comes to the enemy. If you ignore someone
and do not talk about them it is the ultimate insult. Even
though you know he exists, it will be as if he doesn't and
that gives great credit to Jesus. You will give the enemy
the insult he deserves.

Every time Satan had a confrontation with God he
was booted out. Jesus only mentions him on a few
occasions so let us not give too much attention to
Satan. If we are found without our helmet in place we
will be vulnerable to the enemy and he will take the
opportunity to enter our minds. We are capable of
thinking bad thoughts. 'We take every thought captive
to obey Christ' (1 Cor 10:5).

Let us realise that we are capable of thinking bad
thoughts. Some people have had breakdowns blaming
the enemy for their own evil thoughts. If they had recognised their own responsibility in allowing their mind to be
filled with wrong thoughts, taken them to the foot of the
cross and repented of them they would have received
freedom. God gives us a choice: we are free to say 'no'
and we are free to say 'yes'. We are therefore responsible
for our own free will. We are free to go God's way or to
say 'no' to God's way and go our own way. We have
tremendous freedom of choice.

It is not always being tempted or the enemy attack that
causes us to fall. It is often because of our own inward
nature that refuses to come under the control of the Holy
Spirit. One thing we must not do is indulge in self-
deception. It's no good bringing our sins to the foot of

the cross if we do not come as well and make a firm
resolve to leave them there.

We are going to think a little now about what happens
when we deliberately hold on to unforgiveness and
grudges. First, let us consider who it hurts most. The
answer is very simple. If you continue to hold on to an
unforgiveness or a grudge, then the one who is hurt is
yourself. Read the account in Matthew 18 about the unjust
servant and the way he treated his fellow servant who
owed him money. The last verse says this: 'In anger his
lord delivered him to the jailers, till he should pay all his
debts [AV has tormentors]. So also my heavenly Father will
do to every one of you, if you do not forgive your brother
from your heart' (RSV).

We cannot play games with God. If we harbour resentment, unforgiveness or grudges, so also will God hand us
to the tormentors. No one is exempt. The Scripture clearly
states, 'Every one of you'. If we choose not to forgive,
then the Lord will allow us to be handed over to the
tormentors, which in our case would be the alien spirits
or arrows that will find a way into our lives through the
landing strip of unforgiveness or resentment.

It is clear then that we can be our own worst enemy,
allowing Satan a legal right to torment, and if we do not
forgive, then this is what will happen. Forgiveness is part
of the heart of God; it is part of the gospel message. Even
in the Lord's Prayer we have these words: 'Forgive us our
debts, even as we forgive those who trespass against us'.
We also find in other passages that our prayers will not be
answered if we hold anything against our brother.

We also deny Jesus full access into our lives if we are
harbouring unforgiveness. If Jesus does not have full
access into our lives then we deprive ourselves of complete healing and blessing. If we deprive Jesus access then
we also deprive ourselves access to him and all the
blessings he has in store for us. He paid the price on the
cross for us to receive blessing, so then we deprive

ourselves of peace, joy, love, comfort, support and friendship. If we refuse him access we will be the poorer for it,
for we grieve the Holy Spirit, and the Holy Spirit will
stand in the shadow of our life and not be the light of our
life. We will then live in the shadows of uncertainty—in the
shadows of poor and bad events.

If you refuse God access then you are giving permission
for the enemy to play havoc with your life. If God is not
allowed into your life then you are allowing Satan access
again and you are your own worst enemy.

Many of us do not allow Jesus access into areas of our
lives for one simple reason: we do not know how to
receive. We have never learned how to receive. How do
you receive faith? How do you receive love? How do you
receive gifts from God? Some people have been on the
receiving end of bad events so much they have no experience of receiving good gifts and therefore cannot accept.

Ultimately we are the ones who decide whether the
attacks of the enemy are going to affect us or not. Hence
our reason for calling this chapter 'My own worst Enemy:
Myself', for it really is our own choice. We are going to be
in a battle if we are going to stand for Jesus, but it is up to
us how much we allow the attacks to affect us. We have
the freedom of choice.

The very first big battle each of us had was when we
became a Christian and accepted Jesus into our lives for
the first time. Many will remember the tug of war going
on inside as to whether to give way or not; whether, if
we accepted the way of life Jesus offered, we would lose
our friends or whether they would think we were a
religious fanatic. Then when we chose Jesus we found
it was one of the best things we ever did. We chose to
follow him and right through our lives we have to choose
to follow him. If as you read this you are not a Christian,
you may experience the battle right now—the tug inside
that says, 'This is not really true', and, 'don't believe
what you are reading'.

When we say 'yes' to Jesus we are accepting the victory side and the battle is won, but we still have to choose God's way to keep on the victory side. All the way through our Christian lives we choose to allow the enemy to attack us or not. We as Christians need to start to stand our ground and we will not stand unless we make that deliberate choice to do so. We cannot stop the attacks, but we can stop giving Satan the glory. We can deal with them straight away: we can choose to say 'no' and give the glory to Jesus.

We trust that as you read this chapter you will grasp just one truth, and that is the fact that in Jesus you can be victorious if you choose to stand. It is not easy.

The only way you can do this is by walking close to God. It's no good thinking your Christian friends (or your fellowship) will help you stand. These will help you to keep standing, but the ability actually to stand your ground comes from your close relationship with Jesus and your walk with him. In fact we will not be much help to our friends unless we have got a close walk with Jesus first. Many Christians actually drain you because they are not walking close to God first, so they wear other Christians out. We have to tell people when they are like this to go away and feed on God, read his word, pray, seek him. We need to remember our armour and put it on, as we stated at the beginning. Our armour is available for us to use every day–the helmet to protect our thought-life, the breastplate to keep us pure before God.

If we choose to shut off any area of our life then we will be vulnerable to attack, which will wound and hurt. We must not hang on to the secret area. Many Christians hang on to secret areas of sin, which no one knows about, and they think it is hidden, but God knows. We cannot hide our lives from him. While we have a secret life we will never be free and our greatest enemy will be ourselves.

9

Coping with Myself (Control and Manipulation)

One of our greatest enemies is feeling sorry for ourselves. We often call it the 'poor old me's' or the 'poms'. Whatever the name, we certainly can enjoy feeling sorry for ourselves and this alone can cause us harm and hurt. If not dealt with this leads to attention-seeking.

There are many who spend their time seeking attention from other Christians because they want to feel sorry for themselves. If they cannot get what they want from one church they will look elsewhere and leave exhausted people behind them and often bewildered Christians. Some people will go round and round looking for attention but never wanting deep down to be rid of their problems. Their life is not centred on Jesus. They have not chosen to walk close to him first but rather to stick close to other Christians who cannot take the strain and are worn out.

Many of these people have never faced the issues deep down inside and have never let Jesus have the secret hidden depths of their being, hence the true problems are never dealt with and they are an enemy to themselves as well as to their friends. What can we do with these people? This is a question all pastors would long to know the answer to!

First, we need to examine ourselves to make sure we do not fall into the trap of self-pity. Then we have to learn the meaning of the word 'no', otherwise we will fall into the trap of emotional blackmail and always be at their beck and call. Then we have to walk close to the Lord ourselves for words of wisdom and knowledge that will help these folk. Some are always going to be the same because the wounds inside are too deep or too painful and therefore we have to exercise grace and wisdom as did Jesus when dealing with problem people. Sometimes there is a need for true salvation and a recognition of repentance as they begin to see themselves as they really are and understand why they act like they do.

Often we find the only answer is to love these people and accept them as they are because they will be unable to change without a miracle from God. This is often a test to our walk with God as they become like sandpaper rubbing us up the wrong way and causing us to be tested in our weaknesses. We must not wallow in self-pity ourselves. Some people say, 'I have no friends, no one cares for me, I am not wanted and no one visits me', when in actual fact they have put their friends off by their attitude and self-pity.

Often it is the way we are that causes the loneliness and it is like a circle of bad events that needs breaking–only this time it is we who have to break the circle and break the self-pity. Be open to receive rebuke from the Holy Spirit or from your best friend and take heed to what is being said. Your best friend is the one who can tell you the truth about yourself and confirm what God is saying to you and help you through.

Another problem with coping with ourselves is coping with the old records that keep attacking our minds. We have already mentioned this problem, but it is so important to our freedom that we need to mention it again in this chapter. Here is a testimony from a Christian friend who had problems in this area.

'When I was quite young–between the ages ot ten and twelve–I can remember clearly the words 'You are not worth anything', and those words have stuck in my mind ever since, until recently I was freed from them. Those words would go round and round in my mind and it is incredible to think that I really could not get that out of my head for hours at a time. I would go to sleep thinking that. It affects every part of your life as your self-worth is almost non-existent.

'It would give me acute anxiety about little things. I am sure you can remember losing things as a child, but I was constantly losing things – sometimes even a whole bag of things–which meant I would have to go over and over in my mind all the list of things I had lost, and I believe the whole problem was tied up with my lack of self-worth as my mind tried to cope and hence I would lose something else. It was a continual circle of crisis.

'As I grew up there were moments of joy and rage and panic. When confronted with a crowd of people on a tube train I was filled with dread and panic. I would think they were all looking at me and thinking what a worthless person I was. I really found it impossible to sit on tubes and used to stand, looking at the door and pretending I was not there.

'Anxiety stayed with me until I recognised that it needed to be dealt with finally by the Holy Spirit. I have been counselled over a period of time and each time different things have been dealt with and laid to rest and I can testify to the freedom that Christ can bring in the thought-life.'

The one who is in us is greater than any power that is against us and the reason the Lord Jesus came into this world was to break all the power of the evil one. Our weaknesses are able to be overcome in the power of God.

When we are thinking about ourselves we can either think on positive things, and hence sow positive thoughts to our minds, or we can sow negative things and hence negative thoughts. What you sow is what you reap, which is the meaning of Galatians 6. If you sow vegetables in your garden you do not expect to reap flowers, which although nice to look at you cannot eat!

If we sow love we will reap love; if we sow friendship then we will reap friendship. If we begin to sow lies and deceit then we can expect a terrible harvest. I have found that weeds do not have to be planted to appear; they will grow if allowed to and given the opportunity. It is hard work to sow and reap the harvest and it is also true spiritually. We need to take care what we sow 'for in due season we shall reap, if we do not lose heart' (Gal 6:9, RSV). A harvest is assured if we persevere. If we want to reap positive thoughts then we need to mix with positive people.

If we are going to cope with ourselves we also need to understand the 'I want' syndrome which lurks deep down in our carnal nature: I want power; I want domination; I want control; I want to manipulate. Each one of us has something of this nature in us. That is why Jesus died on the cross—so that we could be rid of our old nature. At the foot of the cross we see a picture of what I am sharing: as they gambled the clothes of Jesus the soldiers and the religious leaders shouted out to him, trying to control and manipulate the situation.

Whatever the background cause of this syndrome it is rooted in the dynamic. It is fed on a root of pride. Satan suffered from it. The consequence of this hideous sin was that pride comes before a fall and Satan was kicked out of heaven, and it is no different for us. If we want to have pride, and control and manipulate other people's lives then we too must face the consequences of our sin. It always brings disaster. We have extreme examples today of leaders who have dominated and controlled by evil power, such as Hitler and others who are still dictating in the Middle East.

In the realm of human beings it brings a breakdown of relationships and communication. Either they submit and will not be themselves, or it damages growth and the personal well-being of others because they are always manipulated or controlled by others.

We see it today all over the world where one side tries to control and manipulate the other side. In the former Yugoslavia we have a breakdown of human rights and well-being because there is control being exercised.

Often the root of control is insecurity. If I know where I am and can control the situation then all will be well. Pastors and preachers and church leaders are not above this! Let us be honest with ourselves. We see it in the world of business. We see it among our children when one wants to take control and boss the others around. We call it leadership quality, but leadership qualities that control and manipulate are not God-inspired. In the criminal world we can see control manifested. A criminal will often produce a story in order to create a situation whereby they can get what they want.

Sometimes it springs out of self-preservation, but any attention you give to this will only feed the insecurity and never resolve it. In fact my experience is that if it is not dealt with the person will get worse and this will progress the older they get and the longer it is allowed to go on. In the end they will do it without thinking and the tone of their voice and their body language will be such that if they cannot control they will be so insecure they will not know where they are. If it gets into the church, it will destroy not only the church but the family as well. Whatever its form, whether mild or strong, it is control and therefore alien to God.

God always gives a way of escape. Jesus loves us, but he will also let us go, and if we do not allow people to be themselves and always try to control them then actually we are doing them a disservice. Jesus never did that. He always brought people into freedom, never under domination. He will bring you into subjection, but it is a willing subjection out of obedience because he blesses obedience. He never gets hold of you and tries to manipulate or dominate because he loves you so much.

In 1 Kings 16:19 to chapter 22 you have a whole
episode of control and manipulation by Jezebel and how
she destroyed her husband by her devious methods. She
destroyed not only him but the land and nation.

This power complex is lust. Sometimes it is conscious,
and sometimes unconscious. To oppose this power can
lead to emotional and moral blackmail, which on the
face of it seems quite plausible and you have to be very
smart to see through the facade. Unless you are walking
close to God and have a word of wisdom, you are going to
be hard-pressed to see a way through. If you confront this
evil power you receive an answer which is so clever that
you have difficulty finding a clear way through. It is not
easy and I have been on the receiving end of such a
confrontation in various situations and it has been one of
the most difficult to cope with and awkward to deal with,
especially when dealing with Christians who you know
should know better. Either that or you get an outburst of
comments or remarks that is not easily dismissed or
argued against, which can put great pressure on you. If
you are on the receiving end and you capitulate, then you
may harbour grudges and resentment that will destroy you.

You need to be sure to pray that those who seek to
control have this broken. It means facing insecurity, but
manipulation and control are so rampant in the world, you
can have quiet people who manipulate behind the scenes
or a more forceful character who lays down the law for
you to obey. The ultimate underlying thing is the control
and that is ungodly. Parents can try to control children in
this way by spotting what their children are doing and
planning a manipulative way to catch them out. It's not
righteous. God wants us to be open and honest with our
children if we are going to break this deadly weapon.

Some church members have gone to meetings all pre-
pared to wage war, with their plans and schemes already
worked out, and have manipulated whole meetings and
have changed the whole direction in which the church was

going. This is not of God and has reaped consequences for which they only have themselves to blame.

Often people are unaware that they have been manipulated into making a decision which was pre-planned and schemed hours before. God cannot bless our churches if they are run like this. He cannot look upon sin, so he will leave us to go it alone and await our repentant hearts. It is, I believe, one of the worst enemies to have crept into our churches today–that we have let men and women control and manipulate and have left the church weak and powerless.

Often the pastor is at the receiving end of the control and becomes worn out with trying to confront and keep the whole church clear of evil power. We pray for revival, but there is a lot of self to be dealt with first. There are a lot of leaders, whether they be pastors, elders, deacons or parochial church council, who need to be able to cope with their old sinful nature before God can ever pour out his Spirit on his people in power. The old sinful power has to go and give way to the Holy Spirit to lead and direct. 'Not my way but yours, Lord; not my will but yours.'

If this present move of the Holy Spirit opens our hearts to be totally willing to walk God's way, then we will soon reap fruit and see the true harvest of righteousness being reaped in our lives. We need to be praying against this evil power and seeking to make sure our lives are kept free.

Through the Bible Jezebel is mentioned and whenever this spirit of control and manipulation is there it brings disaster, broken relationships and the disapproval of God.

Ask the Lord who you are hearing. If it is a spirit of control, the 'I want' syndrome takes over your life. If you recognise and can deal with it yourself, then repent and renounce this power and ask God to come and heal you of its effects. Confess the sin and forgive anyone else involved, then renounce the sin and tell God you will no longer allow this to rule your life. Ask a friend who understands to pray for you, or contact us for help. We want to see you set free for the kingdom. As we have stirred the waters and brought up the mud and silt, we allow the fresh cooling waters of the Holy Spirit to wash through.

10

Being Free and Staying Free

It is all very well giving you a book full of instructions on how to be free, but if we do not share how you can stay free, then it will be wasted and forgotten. A lot of the answer concerning how to stay free is found within ourselves. We have written before that God has not made us robots; he has given us a free will and that free will has to be exercised if we are to stay in our freedom. It is a case of choosing to follow the Lord and follow his way. There is always a battle going on, not so much with the enemy in this case, but with ourselves. What we want against what God wants for us.

If we are to keep our new-found freedom in Christ, then we will have to discern more fully his purposes for our lives. We have mentioned on a number of occasions that we are not on this planet to please one another but to please God. George Whitefield, in the last century, came across this problem quite strongly in his ministry. He came to a point where he was falsely accused by both his friends and enemies. He received a vicious letter accusing him of wrong-doing. His reply was brief and courteous: 'I thank you heartily for your letter. As for what you and my other enemies are saying against me, I know worse things about myself than you say about me. With love in Christ, George Whitefield.' He did not try to defend himself. He was much more concerned with pleasing his Lord Jesus.

Paul said, 'If I still please men I would not be a bondservant of Christ'. We need to please God and seek

121

the Lord. It means that there will be times in our lives when we will be misunderstood. There will be times when we are innocent, and the way we react will determine whether we are free in Christ. If we can put the hurt at the foot of the cross and give it over to our Lord and Saviour, we will be a better person, but it is not easy. We must try to avoid being vindictive, because if we are we will lose our freedom in Christ.

Our one desire in life must be to be holy. He must increase and I must decrease. The Christian life should be one of becoming more like Jesus.

A famous musician once noticed in his orchestra a young man whose playing was limited, but he encouraged that young man until one day he realised that he was probably more gifted than he was himself. So he sat in the background and allowed the young man's talent to be seen and heard. That is what Jesus wants from us, so that slowly we will recognise that our ways are nothing compared to his ways and we will let him take control and we will take a back seat.

If we are going to stay free we will need a disciplined life. There is very little discipline in our world today. It is more a case of do your own thing, when you like and how you like. 'I' takes first place. That is why Christian life is so hard compared with the world's way of living. As the Lord sets us free, hopefully we will become a witness and will be asked why we are different.

When we wrote the first chapter we wrote about the armour and as we finish we want to remind you again of the armour. We need to use armour daily. It should be a daily event to make sure it is in order and worn effectively. We never really take it off, but we need to remind ourselves of the spiritual use the armour has and what protection we have. If we feel one day we have failed the Lord, let us repent straight away and confess our sin so that there is not time for condemnation and guilt.

We must keep short accounts! We have everything available to us. Satan has nothing. We are the ones with all the armour and weapons—not him! Our biggest enemy is not Satan, it is ourselves as we ignore the protection which is ours and fall into condemnation instead of keeping short accounts.

We must take time with God. Prayer life and communion with God are important. Your quiet time with God brings life and healing. 'My son, pay attention to what I say; listen closely to my words. Do not let them out of your sight, keep them within your heart; for they are life to those who find them and health to a man's whole body. Above all else, guard your heart, for it is the wellspring of life' (Prov 4:20–23).

We need to pay close attention to what God is saying to us and listen to him. I honestly believe that Christians today have tried another way. Many have received a baptism in the Spirit and they think they can lead the Christian life on gift alone and have forgotten that they need to spend time with the Giver.

The gifts can be tremendous if used with a disciplined life of prayer and reading God's word, but if not then we will misuse them. A lot of havoc today has been caused because Christians are not listening to God. Whole churches have been misled or have not heard aright because their prayer life is so weak or they are looking for movement of the Spirit without first exercising the character of Christ. Many individuals have been wounded and hurt—some so deeply that they have left the church community and are alone. Please take note that if you want to stay free you need to spend time with God and seek his face. We think we can come to church and worship and receive the gifts and that is enough, but we still need a disciplined time with God alone and a relationship with him who loves us. You will need to discipline your life to make room for your time with God.

When we were married the vicar, a dear friend, gave the message. He spoke on the disciplined diary and disciplined quiet time and that we should make time to pray with each other, also have time alone with God. He said we should make time to relax together and with our future family. We have never forgotten that message in thirty years of married life. It has come back to us many times and we have been reminded to take heed of what was said!

We need to learn to hear the voice of God speaking, whether it be to pray or to rest. Sometimes we are so busy with our praying that we neglect the voice of God saying we should rest. That is sometimes why Christians have breakdowns, because they lock themselves into a legal time of prayer which becomes so obsessive that they cannot stop and so wear themselves out when God has told them to stop.

Don't neglect the helmet of salvation and what we wrote about the thought-life being made captive. It is so important today. We may think that we have it easy in the Western world, but if we sit back and think that, then our thought-live will suffer. Our thought-life is where everything begins: temptation, evil thoughts. Our minds are being attacked today in very subtle ways. The mind of the non-Christian is under great pressure from New Age concepts, the occult, and many cults that are seeking mind control. There is a spirit of confusion in the world, so how important it is that we know who our Saviour is and that we know how to follow him closely.

If we allow the Holy Spirit to work through us he can renew our minds. The truth sets us free, but habits are difficult to break and perhaps you have identified a habit which is standing in the way of your walk with God. Please be encouraged to keep going and seek freedom.

If you have an old gramophone record and it gets stuck, it will go round and round in the same groove. Likewise if you have had a habit for many years, then the groove will take time to disappear. You will find yourself having to deal with the old record when it is stuck in that groove.

Take, for example, smoking. It is a habit that cannot easily be got rid of and the only way is to believe that the Lord Jesus can set you free, and to go through the pattern of rejecting the sin and facing the problem before the Lord and asking him to set you free. One day you will wake up and the groove will be gone. To some it happens overnight, but in many cases it is a case of perseverance in taking and confessing before a loving, forgiving heavenly Father who understands. We have to work at staying free and you may need the help of a trusted friend to bring you through. Ask them to pray for you and with you. There is tremendous support in having someone to share with and to openly confess to that you need help. It gives you the will-power that perhaps you need to go on and find victory.

Let us think a little about the temptations that go through our minds. These can be overcome. the Scripture says: 'No temptation has seized you except what is common to man . . .' (1 Cor 10:13). We can overcome temptation. We do not have to give in.

In the world today there is much talk about temptation not existing and that if something feels right we should do it. We as Christians need to face the fact that temptation not only exists but is a powerful weapon to hold us back in our walk to freedom. As Christians we have to learn to resist temptation and that sometimes is not easy. Where another Christian is concerned we have to hate the sin but not the sinner. There is a great temptation to look at another in some sin and criticise them when we should be hating the sin and loving the sinner. We look at the person and criticise them if they are into some sin and say, 'How can they be like that?'

Jesus always loved the sinner but could not look on the sin. He felt sad and had compassion, but he also let them go if they were not willing to repent and seek forgiveness.

He will let us go until we repent. Many are not free in their Christian lives because they have gone their own way and buried their sin of pride or unforgiveness and tried to forget or pretend it does not matter. Before we can come into God's presence we need to seek his forgiveness and cleansing to continue a walk of freedom.

There also has to be some determination in our lives not to give in to temptation. This is not the enemy, and it is our responsibility to say 'no'. Most sin is first desired by us! We choose to fall into the trap or net. Deep down we do not want to say 'no'. If we examine our own motives, we will find that the reason we have a sin or habit that we cannot break (and please note some habits are not sinful) is because we desire that habit or sin. So we need to deny that desire in our minds. Flee from the lust of the flesh (see Jas 1:14–15).

We also need to make sure we do not sin deliberately by saying, 'It won't matter', or, 'No harm will come from it'. If we do this we have opened up a door for Satan to come and play havoc with our mind and emotions. Again we need to deliberately deny the sin, not deliberately do it (Jas 4:17).

Jesus in the wilderness resisted temptation and he asks us to do the same. We need to use God's word as Jesus did as a weapon, a sword to cut through the desire and temptation. There are so many versions of the Bible today that the danger is that we have not hidden God's word in our heart and when the time for action and resisting comes we have no knowledge of Scripture to confront the enemy. The old King James version was poetic and often passages flowed, making it easier to remember. Today we read so many different texts that we find it hard to remember what we have read. Perhaps we need to stick to one version for the sake of learning Scripture. The New International Version is easy both to understand and to remember, so we have quoted mainly from that in this book.

God wants us to know his word and use it for help and support. If you do not find it easy to learn verses of Scripture then find one that really blesses you and keep it with you all the time or put it where you can read it, until it becomes part of you.

Use prayer also as a protection from temptation. Hebrews tells us to pray without ceasing. Prayer needs to become part of our walk with God. It is a way of life. Talk to him when you are walking down the street and when you are waiting for the bus. Seek his guidance and protection in all things so that prayer becomes part of your life. Learn to treat Jesus as a friend.

If you are in the car and you take a wrong turning, thank the Lord. He may have protected you from an accident! It is better than arguing, which is what we used to do years ago. When you go round the roundabout three times, thank the Lord that you missed the car going the other way! God does protect and keep us, and even our mistakes he can take and use for his purposes. Start using your wasted moments for God.

Learn to take the victory over your excuses and weakness. We say, 'I cannot help it', or, 'Well, I am just like that. That's me.' We need to know who we are and what our weaknesses are—not so that they are an excuse, but so that we can give them over to the Lord and begin to mature and grow spiritually. We are not meant to stay spiritually static but to grow and become stronger. God wants us to change to become more like him so that this year's weakness is next year's strength. We will never be perfect, but we can become stronger.

I want to share one of the biggest problems in the world today which is used as an excuse, and sadly by Christians as well, and that is the danger of lying. Lying, however we disguise it, is a sin. A survey done in America recently showed that 91% of those surveyed lie routinely about trivial matters, 36% lie about important matters and 86% lie to family. That is the world in which we live. Lying is causing so much pain and heartache, marriage break-ups, children leaving home, continual abuse and manipulation. As a Christian our desire should be to speak the truth.

I know we could bring up lots of excuses about innocent lies. When I was small, I was sitting in one of the old railway carriages that stretched across so that you sat opposite each other in a line. Opposite me was a lady wearing a hat just like my mother's. In my innocent way I had observed this fact, and to my mother's horror not only stated it out loud but also added how awful it looked! That brings up the type of situation that may make us lie. When someone says, 'Do you like my new dress?' what do you say when you do not like it but feel you must speak the truth? It's then that we ask God for wisdom! We temper truth with mercy.

When I was nursing I was often asked to lie to cover up difficulties and I had to refuse, which meant sometimes I was not popular. Many a time I could have lost my job and on one occasion I was actually given a day off so that I was not around to speak the truth! It protected me so that I was not pressurised to lie. Often we have to make a stand.

Insurance premiums are very high and keep going up because of the increase in crime and in false claims. People are lying and claiming much more than they should. It has even been suggested to us that extra will be added on if we would like so that we could make a bit out of the claim. All this is dishonest and goes on in our world today. If we want to walk free then we cannot be part of any of this. We have to be fools for Christ's sake in the world's eyes. The cost price of being a Christian is sometimes very high, but at the end of the day we have to face our God and it is him we must fear, not man.

Be encouraged to stand firm. Lying causes heartache and deception. What we need to do is stand in our homes and families. We want churches and fellowships where people can come and feel at home and secure, and we will only have that if we walk honestly before God, resisting any form of manipulation or control to gain our own way.

Let us learn to be positive about ourselves, otherwise our minds will become dark rooms where we develop negatives.

To help us not to do this I have written out some responses to certain situations

Negative Response	*Positive Response*
It's all my fault.	It is not all my fault. 'I am forgiven.' I have confessed my sin and Jesus has forgiven me (Rom 8:1).
I am not wanted.	I am wanted. Jesus chose me. I belong to the family of God (1 Cor 12:18).
I don't count.	I do count. I belong to Jesus and am precious to him. He delights in me (Is 42:1 1 Pet 1:18–19).
I must work harder to be accepted.	God's love has no conditions. He sees my life and gives his 'well done' (Mt 25:21).
If I do not make it I will count for nothing.	Because I do count I can be confident I will make it. His grace is sufficient for me (2 Cor 12:9).

These negatives will feed one another so that believing one will emphasise the others. Sometimes it is our fault, but we do not leave it there. We need to confess and repent. If we are at fault, where is the fault when we are forgiven? It has been dealt with at the cross and is no more. Most times we are being led to believe that we are always at fault and therefore will be under pressure to be accepted, and will work harder to convince ourselves that we do count. It is a circle of events that of ourselves we cannot get out of. Do you remember when we were writing about shame and humiliation we noted that a way out was to keep pleasing people, then they will not say something bad about you?

What about our work situation? We are always going to come across someone who can do twice as much work in half the time we can! It leaves us feeling a bit sick or put out. Let's face it, we are going to come across people who work more efficiently than we do. Hopefully we will not meet too many of them!

If we follow this negative pattern then we will be depressed and in despair. We need to take positive steps and realise we are valued and precious to God, even when we are not working at all, saying, 'I am precious, not because of what I have done for God but because Christ died for me'. If we work harder to be noticed by people they will let us work harder but still find fault with us. Most of us want to be wanted and Jesus is the only one who wants us not for what we can do but for who we are in him, precious and chosen. He accepted me and gave me a family. As Christians we will always have a family to turn to.

Often we have genuine negative patterns such as 'I'm so tired'. I know what that is like. I have woken up tired and gone to bed tired! If we are over-stressed and over-tired that is how we shall be and we need to do something about it. If God tells us to stop or slow down, then we are in disobedience if we do not do that. But whatever our situation, we need to turn the tiredness over to him. Jesus is my refreshment and I will give up the right to be tired and will receive my strength from the Lord: 'Come to me, all you who are weary and burdened and I will give you rest . . . my yoke is easy and my burden is light' (Mt 11:28, 30). 'Those who hope in the Lord will renew their strength. They will soar on wings like eagles; they will run and not grow weary, they will walk and not be faint' (Is 40:31).

If we take some of these scriptures on board to combat our negative responses to how we feel, it works.

There is a famous American athlete who actually wrote about waiting on the Lord because he was a very energetic guy on the field. He said that at the first sign of tiredness he started to pray, 'Lord, I'm waiting on you to have my strength renewed and I'm renewing my strength'. Most games he finished as well as he started, because he believed that if he did what God said, it would work. He had to have faith to believe that what God said would come about.

We need to get hold of this. When I was cross-country running I had a prayer: 'Lord, I will put my feet down if you will lift them up!' Many of us at some time have said: 'I cannot cope. I'm not going to make it.' The response we should make to that is: The strength of Jesus is in me so that I can cope. 'If God is for us, who can be against us?' (Rom 8:32). 'I can do everything through him who gives me strength' (Phil 4:13). Please wait until he strengthens you before you do the all things. Sometimes we do the all things before we have been strengthened. We have believed the verse but not waited for the words to be operable in our lives. 'Do not fear, for I am with you; do not be dismayed, for I am your God. I will strengthen you and help you; I will uphold you with my righteous right hand' (Is 41:10).

If you believe that you can, you will. We are not talking about the power of a positive mind, we are writing about the power of being positively renewed through life in Christ.

What about the times when we say, 'No one loves me; no one cares'? I have not often felt like this because I have those who love and care for me, but many do say this. The answer to this is that Jesus loves you. If you are telling yourself about the truth that Jesus loves you, how can you feel unloved?

I often pray for folk for the baptism of the Spirit. A lot of people want to see tongues as the evidence of baptism, but I always ask the person, 'Have you felt something of the love of God?' because if the Spirit of God has been poured into their hearts and he is a Spirit of love, then one of the first evidences I look for is that they are aware of the love of God for them. It should be a personal relationship with their heavenly Father and people who want the baptism of the Spirit just for the gifts are missing the whole essence of the spiritual experience. It is the Giver we need to experience, not the gifts.

Often we hear these words: 'I cannot believe that. It's too good to be true!' Matthew 19:26 says that 'with man this is impossible, but with God all things are possible'. In Luke 1:37 it says: 'Nothing is impossible with God'. We can quote: 'All things are possible to those that believe'. God is greater than any problem that we have to face and he will see us through. We have to choose to believe that and to trust him—a definite choosing on our part to commit ourselves to stay free.

In this closing chapter I want to share some ways of staying free. If you are going through a tough time, then use Scripture like medicine. Take the following prescription three times daily!

1. Confess to God that his word his truth. I remind God of his word.

2. Confess to yourself that his word is true (faith comes by hearing and hearing by the word of God—Rom 10:17).

3. Confess the word of God to the enemy, as the word is the sword of the Spirit. He has no armour, so he does not like the sword!

There are certain verses that I use as spiritual medicine. If an apple a days keeps the doctor away, then a text a day will keep the enemy at bay! I have often done this exercise to build up my faith when life has been difficult.

'Confession' means 'to say the same as' and I have found that saying this three times on different occasions during the day first helps me to remember God's word and hide it in my heart, which helps me not to sin again. Secondly, it builds my faith to receive from God and expect an answer.

Find a Bible you like and stick to that version for remembering.

There are two areas we need to bring to God to keep us walking free. One is those who have sinned against us and the other is those we have sinned against. The best way to forgive is to ask the Spirit of God to come upon you and bring to your memory anyone in these two areas. Write down their names and the event and forgive them one by one and off-load the past and its history, putting it at the foot of the cross where there is an imaginary dustbin and Jesus will carry them away. That will remove a great deal of our past that has played havoc with us and is an exercise we can continue when we need to.

It is very important if we are going to be free not only to off-load but also to forgive ourselves where we have been involved, as we have mentioned before, and this is something we may need to do again. Let us be free from anything that could have an effect on us. I am not saying we should do this every day, otherwise we could become a spiritual hypochondriac, but perhaps every six months, taking a few hours alone with God to examine ourselves and see if we have sinned against anyone or need to forgive someone.

We hear again ringing in our ears, 'Give up; it's no use going on'. Giving up is a habit that has to be broken in the thought-life so that we refuse to give up until God says so. Sometimes we get asked how we survive when we are suffering; how we still look so good! I may look good on the outside, but often am suffering inwardly. I have learned to hold on and not give in and give up while God wants me to hang on. We are victors, not defeatists. God wants us to stand our ground. We are standing for Jesus and it may mean moving our position, remembering we are in God's army which is spiritual and his church is the kingdom of God. As long as we are openly obedient to him we can be blessed whatever happens to us, and wherever he leads us we will follow gladly because inside we are still standing! We do not give up nor give in to the negative thinking and behaviour, but we put our trust in God and move on with him. If we do give in then our Christian life will take a big blow and we will suffer. Obedience is hard at times, but then it was for Jesus. He was obedient even to the cross of suffering and pain. There would be no future for us now if Jesus had not died as he did for our sins.

Another negative that haunts many is: 'I am ugly. I will never be attractive.' The Bible tells you that you are beautiful. In Peter 3:4 we read these words: 'The unfading beauty of a gentle and quiet spirit . . . is of great worth in God's sight'.

If you love someone their face will always be attractive. A long time ago a young lad was being brought up by his mother alone and was conscious that she always wore a veil over her face. He was never permitted to see his mother's face, although she washed him and cared for him and loved him. One day he plucked up enough courage and asked to see her face. 'Why can I not see your face?' he demanded, and she replied, 'But it is so ugly and disfigured, you would not want to see it'. When he was a baby he had been in a blazing fire and she had come in to rescue him and her face was badly burned and scarred. He saw her face for the first time, and with tears in his eyes and love in his heart he kissed his mother's face because he considered it to be beautiful. It represented true selfless love to him.

There is not one of us who if we shine the radiance of Christ through righteous living, will not be considered beautiful. Let no one put you down, for you were made in the image of God.

The Scripture also tells us to confess our faults.to each
other that we may be healed (Jas 5:16). Please note this
says 'faults'. If your translation says 'sins' then it is
wrong. The Greek word means faults. It is not wise for
us to go confessing our sins to each other. We could be a
stumbling-block to someone else. Our faults are not
necessarily sins. Not everyone can handle your confes-
sions and keep them in confidence.

We have a wonderful God. We have a Lord Jesus who
was whole in every part of his life and one of the things
we notice about him is that he took a lot of walks. He
spent a lot of time alone. Regular exercise and fresh air
are common-sense counsel. Please have sufficient rest
and recreation. Leisure pursuit is not wrong. We also
need to take note of what we eat. A sensible diet is
important.

If posible we need to avoid over-fatigue and stress, but I
write this knowing that even I find this almost impossible
in the daily routine of life today. It is a battle we constantly have to face and the only way is to take time out
and away. If we are in a very pressurised job then we will
need more time out to compensate. It is a very hard fact
today that loss of jobs and competition for work have
caused no end of pressure for those in work to keep their
job. Sometimes it is better to risk being out of work than
risk a heart attack which will take you out of work any-
way.

I trust that you will look for friends who will support
you to think positively and therefore remain free. We
should not be loners. We can jog alone, run marathons
alone, but we cannot live alone. We may live by ourselves,
but we need friends to love and support us, for that is how
God intended us to live.

If you want to climb the ladder to spiritual success then
learn to climb downwards! The Christian life, to be a
success, is to move downwards to servanthood. The greatest are those who have humbled themselves before God.

If we have the word of God dwelling in our hearts then we will feel secure and be able to walk free and stay free.

As we close we want to encourage you to desire to walk close to Jesus and obey his voice. As we finish this book we are very aware that God is shaking his church today and he is bringing a godly fear back into the lives of Christians.

For too long now we have blamed the enemy or feared him more than we fear God. God is to be feared, and by that I do not mean we are to be afraid but we are to reverence and respect him because he is able and the most powerful in the universe. He does hold everything together and he is watching over this world, even though his heart must still bleed at the disobedience of man. The time will come, and I am sure it is not far away, when every knee shall bow and every tongue confess that he is Lord. He is waiting for his glorious bride the church to be ready and adorned for him as she walks in holiness and uprightness before him.

APPENDIX ONE

Our Holy Spirit Experience

This final chapter has been added as a direct result of what has happened to us personally since writing this book. It backs up what we have been writing and shows that God is wanting to bring about holiness in our lives, and bring us all to a place of obedience in him where we can effectively be used for the kingdom of God.

About eighteen months ago, we laid down pastoral ministry in a very busy area of the inner-city of London. Why did we do this? We believe it was a direct result of our desire to seek what was God's will for our lives and our desire to walk in obedience to that. We had been seeking the Lord for some time about our ministry. We were tired. We had given of ourselves to see the kingdom established and were praying earnestly for a breakthrough in the church or in our own lives. Then the Lord gave Chris a clear vision. This is what he saw and what he believes the Lord was saying to him.

'I saw a large cliff, too big to climb or to get around. I commanded the cliff to move in the name of Jesus. The cliff then broke into smaller pieces before my eyes. In my imagination I tried to move the debris still opposing my way through, but to no avail. It was too big a task for me. I then asked the Lord to show me the significance of what I could vividly see in my mind's eye. He then showed me a whole team of people moving the boulders and I saw the value of team ministry. He then showed me I needed to lay down the ministry, for the people required to move the rubble had to learn to do it themselves without my help.'

At the same time as Chris had this vision we had disturbing news from one of our children, which again clarified our need to stop and evaluate our lives and our future.

So what next? We had several offers of help and places to go, but the one that seemed right to us was from a Christian retreat home in Bungay, where we had friends. We were offered a small flat where we could live as a temporary home and I would help on the team and Chris would be free to have a sabbatical and we could seek the Lord together. So we laid down everything and went to Norfolk.

The week we resigned we had a phone call from two different brothers suggesting we hung on a little longer and went to Toronto where, they had heard, amazing things were happening, especially to leaders in our position.

It sounded tempting, but we knew God had already spoken to us and if he wanted us in Toronto he would open up the way. One thing we did do was to ring Chris' brother in Toronto who at that time was a backslider and ask him to check this place out. We will tell you the results of that phone call later!

So we resigned and packed up all our earthly possessions, leaving most of them stored in the church house and taking with us only necessary items. Arriving at Bungay, in East Anglia, we settled into a totally different way of life. Chris was able to complete a thesis that he had been struggling to finish for years, and both of us were able to really seek the Lord and pray and listen to what God was saying. We knew this was only a temporary stay and so our future was really in God's hands.

Our time in Bungay coincided with the Holy Spirit blessing the small fellowship called Hillside Fellowship.

So we began to experience a blessing from God. Our first experience was when we attended the mid-week prayer meeting which ended up in uncontrollable laughter. Now Chris and I can laugh, as many of our friends would tell you, this but was different. It bubbled up inside like a fountain and just had to be released! We returned to our small flat and got on our knees, put our heads in our pillows and continued to laugh in a spiritual fashion!

We began to look for fruit from our experience. We certainly felt different, but there seemed to be no tangible result. A few days later I was preparing lunch in the kitchen and was busy slicing runner beans when I happened to look up and there, at almost eye level, was a very large spider hanging upside down. You may ask what significance that had. All my life I have been terrified of spiders. In fact it was a phobia, which meant I had no control over my reactions. I would scream hysterically, often run, or worse hit out at others in my way. You can now appreciate my amazement when I found myself confronting this spider with hardly any fear whatsoever—just a feeling of dislike. Over the years in prayer ministry I have sought release and have controlled my feelings up to a point, but the gripping fear underneath was still there. Now I felt different. I just carried on preparing the beans. Suddenly the spider dropped into the basket of beans. At this point my husband came into the kitchen and I calmly said, 'There is a large spider in my runner beans'. His reply was, 'It wants to do the eight-legged race'.

Now to face my fears was one thing, but to have a joke made was something else! Normally I would have reacted with something like, 'How dare you make fun when you know how afraid I am!' Instead I found myself laughing and I realised some deep healing had taken place that only God could do. I was released from my phobia. I still disliked the creature and could not pick it up, but I could now ask another person to remove it for me in a kindly fashion without hysterics.

The other interesting feature about phobias is that they make you fear other people's reactions as well. In my case this came from childhood when at a youth meeting I was chased by a boy threatening to put a spider down my neck. The fear in me was so great that I threw a large chair at him with full force which could easily have injured him if it had hit him direct. There is a lesson here to teach people to respect others' fears, especially children. I was not released from the fear of people's reactions because I could control my own. This healing was to have great significance in our future!

Several months after Chris started his sabbatical he flew out to Guyana in South America to teach in the Bible school and to visit some of the pastors for Philip Mohabir, who has planted well over sixty churches in Guyana. While he was away I continued my help at Quiet Waters, the Christian retreat centre. It was not easy letting Chris go for five weeks to such a remote part of the world where there were always dangers. As he left and I saw the back of the car disappearing down the drive, a thought came into my mind that I may not see Chris again. I discovered when he came back that Chris too had had such thoughts.

The team at Quiet Waters kept me going and one day asked me why I did not go with Chris. I immediately answered with a whole host of excuses from the heat, to my health and of course my fear of spiders! I did qualify it by saying that if God gave me a very clear call I would go, but it would have to be a real bolt from heaven!

One night, when I had finished taking the evening epilogue, I was again challenged by the thought that Chris may not come back. I had been sharing the story of Shadrach, Meshach and Abednego, when they refused to worship anyone but God and were thrown into the fiery furnace. The part I was particularly wanting to share was the fact that they were willing to go into the fiery furnace, confident that God would rescue them, but even if he did not they would still trust in him. This to me showed real faith–to trust even when things do not go your way or when everything else fails and your faith is still strong.

As I went up to bed that night a voice came very clearly into my mind: 'Would you really trust God if Chris did not return?' I knew the enemy was trying to get at me, but he must have had permission from God to do so! I examined myself for nearly two hours. I knew in my head that I would still trust, but I needed to say 'yes' with my heart as well. After I had battled with my thoughts for what seemed a very long time I said, 'Yes, Lord. You know I would trust you. I would need you even more.' As I verbalised my thoughts I felt a new release and peace flood my whole being. I felt great, I had given Chris over to the Lord and if he did not come back I would face the situation with a new-found courage and strength.

The other area God had been laying on my heart while I was alone was my family. I felt God was burdening me to pray for the way to open up for us to return to our home in Birmingham so that we could be near our children and grand-children. This I knew was a desire of my heart, but I kept it to myself until I knew it was the way we should go. I began to pray for confirmation and direction. Most of our ministry has been in London and if this was the place we were being called to I could not see how the two matched up.

There was great rejoicing when Chris was returned to me in one piece, and as we shared experiences, I found he had been in danger, having nearly lost his life falling off a gang plank into a small boat on a rather large and danger-ous river. We thanked the Lord for bringing us back together and then began to plan our next trip overseas, which was to be of great significance to us.

Chris' brother emigrated to Canada some twenty-nine years ago, and in that time had been far away from the Lord. When we heard what was going on at Airport Vineyard we asked Richard to go and investigate. His first reaction was negative–he could not find any evidence that anything was happening and said he had no idea where the church was! Then a few weeks later we had another phone call to say he had found the church and it really was a move of God.

He had come back to the Lord and was now regularly attending the services. He then said we should come out ourselves and booked us flights, sending us the tickets! So we were to spend Christmas with Richard, plus visiting the Airport Vineyard church. As Richard was now committing himself to the fellowship we became closely linked to what God was doing and were able to stay for three weeks!

Our trip out was quite eventful. A few days before we were to go, I hit my head on a concrete lintel as I descended the cellar steps. It must have knocked me a bit senseless because I was not aware of anything until the blood dripped over my glasses! We were leaving the next morning for a final visit to family, so had little time to worry about my head and really prayed for the Lord to heal. The problem was, I was also suffering from the effects of flu, so by the time we had travelled to our son in Birmingham I was really unwell, and lay on their sofa thinking, 'I cannot go a step further!' I was duly prayed for again and bundled into the car to go to my father-in-law's cottage, where we were to spend the night before going to leave our car at our cousin's near the airport. I fell into bed thinking I could never fly the next day. As it was, I was still not completely clear from my fear of flying, so being sick did not help that either!

I awoke the next morning, amazed to find the sickness had vanished and I was well apart from feeling somewhat weary. It was now Chris' turn for attack! We had just left visiting his dad and had about an hour before driving off, when his spectacles fell off onto the ground and one arm broke off! The problem was he could not drive without them and I could not drive his car!

We walked to every optician, with no success, and then I decided it was time for my nursing experience to come into action. Having acquired some tape and a small stick I duly began to splint and bandage the side of his specs! It worked, and Chris looked a real spectacle at the airport with this large white bulge around his glasses! I just prayed they would not think it was suspicious and start to strip it all off. I am glad to say they were also amused.

We had by this time realised we really were being attacked and started seriously to claim our victory, and Jesus as Lord. The psalmist does say that we as the righteous will go through many troubles, but the Lord will deliver us from them all.

We had one more trouble left and that was Chris' suitcase, which decided it had had enough and burst its zip! We had to borrow his cousin's and re-pack. That seemed nothing compared with all the other hassle.

It was a great relief to arrive in Toronto Airport and see our brother waiting for us. Praise God we had made it, even if we did look like two war victims!

Our first week at the Airport Vineyard was to be very significant to us. I was obviously very tired and spent most of the first few days lying on the carpet. The Lord was doing a healing work in me and I just enjoyed his presence. No one prayed for me, it was just a precious time with God. I had been spoken to the first Sunday by a word on forgiveness. It was not so much choosing to forgive, but a forgiveness from the heart when you bless the person who has offended you–in fact to bless them with a blessing they do not deserve. I found this very hard when someone had hurt one of our children deeply. To forgive that person I knew was right as a Christian, but to bless them was a very difficult thing to do, and yet I knew God was speaking to me and telling me to bless him. The Lord said that if I did not it would be like a milestone around my neck and so in my pain I learned a deep lesson of forgiveness from the heart. For then the Lord showed me how his Son had forgiven mankind for the way they had hurt and abused him. True forgiveness is a choice of the will and an act of the heart.

In the meantime amazing things were happening to Chris. Chris never went down in the Spirit–in fact he had iron legs–so when I could not find him I still did not believe that was where he was, until his brother told me! Chris continues the story.

It is impossible to describe all that happendd because so much occurred. However, the fruit are evident from all the wonderful experiences and events of our Toronto visit. This of course must be the real test of any experience: does it lead to greater love for Jesus and fruitfulness of the Holy Spirit? There are a number of other evidences one should look for, and these will emerge a little later.

Before testifying to the way in which God met me, let me state my perceptions of the folk and meetings at Toronto. There is no deliberate hype in the worship or other times to create a high dramatic emotional atmosphere to gain a response from people. Many of the meetings were little different in many ways from low-key charismatic or free evangelical services. This I found very reassuring. Naturally during the ministry time there were some sights and sounds that seemed strange, but despite that it was always clearly evident that the Holy Spirit was working.

The ministry time of prayer was always conducted in a worshipful manner. In fact the musicians played quiet worship songs to retain the atmosphere of worship and reverence. This also I found reassuring.

The men leading the services, speaking and sharing, were all clearly men of grace, true humility and honesty, with a genuine desire for the people of God to be blessed with the power of the Spirit to honour the Lord Jesus Christ.

Now let me share some of my personal experiences with you. The first evening I was prayed for I felt nothing at all, even though a number of relevant issues were prayed for by several people on the Vineyard ministry team. These included being filled with and released by the Spirit, also for the chains and shackles to be broken, such as inhibitions. Therefore, as I stood waiting upon the Lord, I asked him why I had felt no emotions at all, even though I had reached out in trust to him. In dialogue I felt the Spirit ask me how I had been saved at conversion. My response was, of course, 'By faith'. The Lord then told me that this was how it would be for me. As I exercised faith I would receive and then have the corresponding feelings following.

The next time I received prayer was on Christmas Day. Just the day to have presents from the Lord as you again vow to give yourself to him as a gift for him to use as he wills. It was evident that there would be no prayer ministry as such on Christmas Day as the service closed. However, I marched forward, clambered onto the platform, tugged the senior pastor's arm and asked for prayer. Very graciously John Arnott directed me to one of his associate prophetic pastors who began to pray then prophesy over me. Without expanding what was said prophetically, all has come to pass and is therefore true, but more importantly it confirmed all that the Lord had been speaking to me about and which I had not shared with others. Perhaps two things can be shared.

First, I had a record of unfulfilled prophecies and these were about to be fulfilled. In fact I actually had in my Bible a word given to me some eleven years previously.

Secondly, I would have a ministry that would speak to more people than I imagined, for it would expand. Several days later Jean and I were interviewed for a United States Christian television programme. This has now been broadcast in the USA and was most likely beamed across the Caribbean. I don't think this was quite the fulfilment but it certainly spoke to us!

Perhaps the most surprising thing was that after these and other prophetic words were spoken, I went down under the influence of the Holy Spirit for the very first time. I floated down like a feather, absolutely weightless, totally peaceful with a deep feeling of being secure. While on the floor, I had a vision of a hose-pipe hosing me down with fresh water from head to toe. Asking what this meant, I received the reply, 'I am hosing down past generations and cleansing them, so that you are free from the past'. I felt that what I had received on Christmas Day was like being handed a present and that there were things to unwrap from the present.

The way I felt when being prayed for was not always the same, although most times were quiet and restful, warm and secure. On a few occasions I did go down again and these produced quite different sensations, although quite pleasant.

Two further experiences chosen from a number need to be shared. The first was while standing and the Spirit of God took me through various stages of my life from birth onwards. The stage of my mid-twenties took me back to the death of my first son Simon, when he was just a year old. The pain and anguish in my chest and emotions were so extreme I broke into crying and weeping as the Lord ministered his healing and the pain was released. I then asked the Lord if there was anything else he wished to show me from this experience. 'Yes', he said. 'This is how I felt when my only Son died.' Again I cried. Once more I asked if there was anything to learn from this. This time I felt the Lord was saying that he felt like this over those of his creation who rejected his Son, so making for them his sacrifice something wasted. This gave me a deep inner insight and awareness of the Father's heart for me in his love and tender merciful grace. The final stage, my present one and in the future, was bathed in golden light of love, security and fulfilled promise. I saw a prophet warrior clad in gentleness and love.

The final experience to share can be called a Naaman experience. This particular night I felt I needed to be prayed for seven times and that on the seventh I would receive a special blessing. Just as Naaman was told to bathe seven times in the Jordan River to be rid of his leprosy, and only gained freedom from his malady on the seventh wash, so also I believed there would be something special the seventh time I was prayed for.

After six times it was late and the many members of the ministry team were leaving. In fact I had to grab someone to pray for me as they were leaving for home with their families. It was the prophetic pastor. He said the Lord was calling me to be a warrior and that my anointing would increase. He also said that I would be a warrior among the nations and that the gift of faith was being given. Interesting was the fact that during the meeting I saw, as it were, Elijah and Elisha walking together on the occasion that Elijah was to be taken by God. I saw the prophetic mantle fall to the ground and I saw myself pick it up. The prayer ministry of this brother, along with the vision I had seen, only confirmed yet again my prophetic ministry for God. In terms of finance, God would lead us from one source to another so that Jean and I could fulfil the work here and overseas that he had called us to.

Jean continues with her experiences. I was still enjoying 'carpet ministry' each day when Chris called me over to Jim, who had been praying for him. I thought he wanted to introduce me, but he wanted to pray over me. This was a major turning point in my life. Chris was instructed to hold me up while Jim began to prophesy. Poor Chris, I am not a light person and what I was hearing was knocking me out! I could hear myself crying out inside, 'No, Lord, not that!'

You may recall that a few months back I was asked why I did not go with Chris to Guyana and I related all the good reasons why I would not go, qualifying it with, 'But if God really spoke to me I would have to go'. Here was God now, confirming through prophecy our future ministry, including in it a strong place for me beside my husband. Wherever God would lead we were to be together and Jim said he saw me ministering to 'Indian-type people', to which Chris quickly replied, 'That's Guyana!' He said many other things as well, such as God being pleased with me, which I was relieved to hear! Also that I would be like a curtain opening the Holy Spirit to people's lives. That was confirmed again when we returned to Norfolk by a girl we had prayed over and asked for her to hear God more clearly. When she got up from the floor she told me God had given her a picture of a curtain, although she did not understand it, but I did!

Jim also answered some of the queries that had been going on in my mind, such as where the money would come from. He said the Lord would provide, and up till now he has in various ways. He said I was to look after Chris' diary, something I really enjoy doing because I can put in all the holidays and days off and family days we believe we should have! He imparted wisdom and discernment and words of knowledge in greater measure and all these we have found more prominent in our ministry since we have returned.

The major change in my life came when I realised God was calling to me to visit and minister for him in Guyana and perhaps some of the other Third World countries. All the fears that had lain dormant surfaced, and for the next few days I lay on the floor shaking with what I am sure was fear, knowing in my heart I wanted to obey the Lord at all costs and yet the reality was hitting me.

Then I had a wonderful experience as the Lord gave me a vision. If you have ever been to Niagara Falls you will know that at the top of the falls there is an area of river where you are warned not to go beyond, for it is the point of no return. If you do you will go over the falls and most likely lose your life.

In this vision, I was thrown into those very waters and I knew there was no return. I began to shake with fear as I realised I was going over the falls, and then just as I was about to fall a pair of hands lifted me up and held me. It was Jesus, and the words 'Perfect love casts out fear' came into my mind'. Perfect love is the love of Jesus, who will go to any lengths to save us and keep us from falling.

My fears left me and I stood up a different person, ready to go anywhere for him. I could now put into place all that God had been dealing with in the past months: my letting go of Chris, my phobia of spiders healed, my fear of flying overcome. Now he had shown me he was there for me in a very real way.

The next night I was so full of joy and boldness I shot out to the front to share a testimony to several thousand folk, and it was very encouraging to find later that Mary, who was speaking, was actually speaking on the water and the river flow! Chris and I had more 'carpet ministry' out the front and then we dissolved into laughter. I think it was just release and joy, knowing God was speaking into our lives. The laughter was all over the building that night making it hard for Mary to speak, but God was doing a real work among us all.

If you think Toronto is all fun and laughter you are mistaken. God is preparing his church and his people for the future, and some nights were really heart-rending.

It was two nights later that God started to speak to us again. Ron from the States was speaking about laying down our lives and obviously this excited us because that was what God was showing us. It was a very serious message and hit home to us as he mentioned South America, which is where Guyana is, and he mentioned a friend laying down his life for Jesus and how revival sometimes involves martyrdom.

As we listened, I knew God was reaching into my heart and I felt fear arise again. It was not that I believed God was asking us to be martyrs but that we would be willing to lay down everything, and that included our lives, for his sake. I began to battle with this one. I had given Chris over to the Lord, but self-preservation was very strong in me.

As the altar call came Chris was ready to go out and I dragged behind, knowing that I had reached the point of no return, yet afraid of what that might mean. As God touched me again he healed something in me and my fears again left and I felt wonderful.

It was just as well, for straight afterwards we were interviewed by *Charisma* magazine that has programmes on American TV. So my testimony went out across America and into South America on 7th March 1995. They did not know it, but it was a very significant interview! God had blessed me, he had touched me, he had changed me. I would never be the same again. My prayer life has grown, my desire to read the word has grown, my ability to hear his voice is much clearer. I have a new boldness for the Lord, and even months later my attitude has not changed. What God did and is doing is lasting. Hence our reason for writing this Appendix. All that has happened to us just emphasises what we have written about even more and shows that God is into inner healing in a very real way today.

Since our return we have moved back to be near our family and have set up a base from which we can work and travel. The Lord is opening doors all the time for us and we are sharing and teaching healing as well as Chris writing Bible correspondence courses to help in Guyana.

We trust you will see lives changing all around you and will also seek the Lord and find that his Spirit can reach into the depths of your heart and change you for his glory. Amen.

APPENDIX TWO

Prophecies and Explanations

When the enemy comes in like a flood, the Spirit of the Lord will put him to flight.

There is a counterfeit move of the Spirit moving alongside the true move of the heart. This counterfeit also has manifestations and only those with a true discernment of spirit can pick up the counterfeit. It is an arrogant, proud spirit attached to Jezebel and has a mocking attitude to the things God is doing in people's lives.

The true Spirit is of the heart, where the heart changes in complete obedience to the Father heart of God, changing lives, bringing a work of grace into the person. Their fruit will bring blessing.

What does God want us to do concerning the counterfeit? Leave well alone. Let Satan hang himself; let the counterfeit crash. God will take care of his sheep. He is a sovereign God and well able to deal with Satan.

He asks those of us who are aware to pray for the protection of people who seek the true River of life. Nothing will or can stop what God is doing. Pray for more discernment for leaders to recognise where Satan is at work and send him packing!

Those whose hearts are truly seeking God will not receive any counterfeit but will actually begin the work of destruction as their hearts are changed.

There is no need to fear. Keep receiving from God, and he will keep you in his love. If you are seeking God with all your heart then that is who you will receive. If your eyes are on what Satan is doing and not Jesus, then you will see things that put fear into you.

The counterfeit spirit cannot be isolated to one denomination or one leader. Like God's Spirit he is working everywhere, even when we meet at a conference to discuss his work. Wherever there is hidden sin, hidden agendas and double-minded people, the enemy will latch on. His days are running short. He is working as hard as he can to stop this powerful move of God and the only way to stop him is to allow God to captivate our hearts and to receive revelation and discernment to lead us to prayer and intercession.

Jean Bristow, 21st January 1995

I saw a picture of a powerful river and along its banks on either side were tall trees reaching down to the water's edge. The Lord seemed to be saying to keep close to the river and its flow, for away from the river are black, dead trees; no life, only dead, black tree stumps. Even the new shoots that appeared from time to time would die off if they stayed away from the flow.

The power of the enemy will be manifested in the darkness and the barren land, but where the river of the Spirit touches just the roots of the tree there will be new life and new growth. The tree will flourish and no amount of testing and trial from the enemy will touch the river of life nor those close to the flow whose roots are being fed daily and whose lives are committed to the task of serving and reigning. The river of life is Jesus. The hearts of those committed will be hearts that beat and throb with his heart and desire only to serve him.

To some, God may be saying that they need to move physically to keep in the flow of God's Spirit. To others there is plenty of room on the banks. Stay put and put your roots down deep into the flow of God's love. Don't wait for the flow of the river to come to you. The roots of the tree seek out the water. A river takes its own course and you need to follow and find the blessing so that the tree can grow and flourish. If you just wait you could be passed by. Seek and you will find; knock and the door will be opened unto you. (See Is 43:18–21; 48:17; 44:3–5.)

Jean Bristow, December 1994, Toronto

Picture of a garden

Jesus is welcoming you and me into his garden, but he does not just walk through. He stops at each flower and asks us to look into the beauty of each different flower Father has created. He asks us to smell the scent and the fragrance; to stop on a little bridge and gaze into a still pool full of beautiful water-lilies; to feel the peace and the tranquility of his presence.

I believe the Lord is saying to us 'Come into my presence and stay there long enough to receive the Father's heart'. Often your mind is on other things. You want to move on and Jesus wants you to stay with him; to enjoy what he is sharing with you; to receive his peace and his love and his compassion, and as you receive, when you go out from his presence much of the fragrance of Jesus will go with you into a world that has no idea of the beauty Father has made. There is a battle to stay in the garden. It's not easy to stay still with the Lord. It is easier to be doing, and often we are anxious to be doing rather than receiving. Stay with him. He wants to bless you.

Jean Bristow, Intercessors' meeting, 3rd January 1995, Toronto